United Methodist Women

Supportive Community
1992

GodDependency

D0967181

GodDependency

Finding Freedom from Codependency and Discovering Spiritual Self-Reliance

Lynne Bundesen

CROSSROAD • NEW YORK

1991

The Crossroad Publishing Company
370 Lexington Avenue, New York, NY 10017

Copyright © 1989 by Lynne Bundesen

All rights reserved. No part of this book may be reproduced, stored in
a retrieval system, or transmitted, in any form or by any means,
electronic, mechanical, photocopying, recording or otherwise, without
the written permission of The Crossroad Publishing Company.

Library of Congress Cataloging-in-Publication Data

Lynne Bundesen.
 GodDependency: finding freedom from codependency and discovering
spiritual self-reliance / Lynne Bundesen.
    p. cm.
    ISBN 0-8245-0952-8
    1. Co-dependence (Psychology) - Religious aspects.
    2. Spiritual life. I. Title II. Title: GodDependency.
RC569.5.C63B86 1989
616.86 - dc20   89-35846
                                                              CIP

The women and men who brought codependency to public attention, and Robert and Cynthia Heller, Stephanie, and the members of Twelve Step programs, particularly those in Lynchburg, Virginia, deserve special thanks for their part in this book.

And Wilhemina and Ed elevated and supported the work beyond any thanks that I can give them.

CONTENTS

Preface

This book is about understanding God for yourself.

It is about the difference between codependency and dependence on God. Dependence on God is defined as spiritual self-reliance.

Codependency means many things to many people, but generally refers to a mental climate and a certain set of behavior responses brought about by exposure to addiction. A codependent is one who is involved with or dependent on someone with an addiction problem—alcohol, drugs or other dysfunctional behavior.

Over fifty million people in this country were raised in homes ruled by alcohol and as a result suffer from certain adaptive behavior patterns which cripple their ability to live life abundantly—if at all.

GodDependency is about living life abundantly. It is not another form of codependency. Dependence on God means the relinquishment of all forms of socially adaptive codependent behavior. It means relinquishing an addicted, codependent self in order to find your own unique and healthy and sacred God-dependent, God-related, spiritual self.

This book views the symptoms of codependency as invitations to discovering spiritual self-reliance, and views addiction and codependency as cries for spiritual help which can be answered by an individual understanding of God.

Recognizing the symptoms of codependency is important in the same way that it is important to recognize any disease or destructive pattern of behavior. Fruitless patterns repeat themselves. If the fruitless pattern of codependency is not recognized it continues unchecked and untreated and unhealed. Recognized, codependency can be dealt with and can lead the psyche to demand a more practical, cogent explanation of the role of God in daily life. In turn, this can lead to churches which address the issues raised by codependency.

One perspective of this book observes that the Twelve Step meetings of Alcoholics Anonymous are issue-oriented churches. This book is for you if you are in a Twelve Step program and are exploring an understanding of God.

Another perspective of this book is that denominational religion has much to do to match the recognition, management and healing that comes to addicted and codependent people in AA meetings. This book is for you if you are in a denominational religion or are interested in the Bible and in studying it seriously.

Both perspectives meet in the common sentiments and attitudes expressed in the Twelve Steps of Alcoholics Anonymous and in the prayer that Jesus gave when asked "How do we pray?" It is commonly referred to as The Lord's Prayer.

The Twelve Steps are laced through with the importance of individual reliance on God; with forgiveness, and action based on forgiveness. They recognize the need for deliverance from evil.

The Lord's Prayer begins with an acknowledgement of the universality of God as parent, and addresses forgiveness and deliverance from evil. This book discusses an individual understanding of God, forgiveness and deliverance from self-destructive behavior in individuals and society.

As a guide to the issues discussed in this text the following two pages contain the Twelve Steps and the Lord's Prayer.

The Twelve Steps of Alcoholics Anonymous*

We admitted we were powerless over alcohol—that our lives had become unmanageable.

Came to believe that a power greater than ourselves could restore us to sanity.

Made a decision to turn our will and our lives over to the care of God as we understood Him.

Made a searching and fearless moral inventory of ourselves.

Admitted to God, to ourselves, and to another human being the exact nature of our wrongs.

Were entirely ready to have God remove all these defects of character.

Humbly asked Him to remove our shortcomings.

Made a list of all persons we had harmed, and became willing to make amends to them all.

Made direct amends to such people wherever possible, except when to do so would injure them or others.

Continued to take personal inventory and when we were wrong promptly admitted it.

Sought through prayer and meditation to improve our conscious contact with God as we understood Him, praying only for knowledge of His will for us and the power to carry that out.

Having had a spiritual awakening as the result of these steps, we tried to carry this message to others, and to practice these principles in all our affairs.

Reprinted with permission.

The Lord's Prayer

Our Father in heaven,

Your name be revered!

Your kingdom come!

Your will be done

On earth as well as in heaven!

Give us today bread for the day,

And forgive us our debts, as we have forgiven our debtors.

And do not subject us to temptation,

But save us from the evil one.

(Matthew 6: 9–13, *The Bible: An American Translation*)

This book is divided into two parts.

In Part One you will hear the voices of men and women who themselves are and have been addicted and codependent. Part Two offers a workbook section designed for use with the Bible. The workbook gives suggestions on how to develop and practice an understanding of God and how to practice spiritual self-reliance.

In the past decade, as the emphasis on growth of the individual self has become a major influence in western public consciousness, the term *codependent* has been used in books and lectures, on television shows and in the daily conversation of many people in this country.

Millions of people in the United States and throughout the world are working through the steps of recognition and recovery from codependency. Many of them are members of Alcoholics Anonymous-related Twelve Step programs and are trying to define God as they understand God. These men and women have discovered that addiction is in the very atmosphere of the nation and that there is a practical value and deep comfort and relief from codependency in discovering GodDependent spiritual self-reliance.

This book explores the role of the addict and codependent in AA meetings and in denominational religion.

I am a journalist who, for the past decade, has written exclusively on religion and its impact on individuals, government and social issues. For five years I wrote a weekly newspaper column on religion and I interviewed the leading ministers and theologians of our time. As a journalist I interviewed hundreds and hundreds of people who call themselves codependents. I attended countless numbers of Twelve Step meetings in several parts of the United States. I read all the literature and conducted more interviews and spent a year in research on this issue.

But this book is a not a full discussion of codependency. For those who want to know more about the subject there are books by experts in this field that explore the symptoms and attitudes of codependents in great detail. Most every book store has a shelf full of such books.

Neither is *GodDependency* a full discussion of how God comes to human consciousness, how to recognize the kingdom of heaven in yourself, how suffering brings healing, how a nation matures—all subjects that interest me and are an outgrowth for me of my study and research.

Rather this book is a first step in the discussion of what codependency has to do with your relationship to God. It is a book designed to have a practical application for anyone looking for a better personal understanding of God.

It is a book that calls into question some popular codependent and theological notions and is meant to raise issues for discussion in churches and AA-related meetings.

Chapter One tells you something about me and my codependency and what I think of the issue. Chapter Two will tell you—if you haven't already heard—something about the current definitions of codependency and Chapter Three gives some human examples. Chapter Four discusses how reliance on God—Spirit—brings spiritual self-reliance and gives some examples of its attitudes and Chapter Five is a discussion of the nature of the God or Higher Power who "heals all our diseases."

Chapter Six is about how GodDependency fits into AA and the Twelve Steps and about where we might, as individuals and as a nation, go next in understanding ourselves.

Part Two is a workbook section for use by the individual—of any age and in any circumstance—looking for a specific and individual sense of God in daily life. In Part Two you will find applications of an understanding of God to some specific symptoms of codependency. The applications are derived from definitions of God found in the Old and New Testaments, and they are offered as guides to spiritual self-reliance.

I hope this book will find its way into the hands of the clergy and church members and any individual looking for a way out of hell and for a more satisfying understanding of God and healing.

This book is for you if are interested in spiritual freedom, in a God that helps you understand who you are now. I hope it suggests to you your own, individual, powerful, timeless, God-related identity and causes you to reflect on some of the issues raised by codependency.

This is not a book from an ivory tower. It is a book by

someone who has lived those issues and is committed to the development of spiritual self-reliance.

Part One

GodDependency

1

Confessions of a Codependent

I am a codependent. Or at least that's what people who are working on their codependency tell me.

I didn't know that I was codependent—in fact I didn't know any more about codependency as a syndrome or pattern of behavior than I had read and heard in print and on television—until an acquaintance said that I had all the classic symptoms of a codependent.

Number one on my list of classic symptoms, according to my friend who attended AA Twelve Step meetings, was that I didn't go out very much, if at all. I thought that the reason I didn't go out was because I like to stay home and believe there is a real value in being at home. I also thought that I stayed home because that is where my computer is and I had work to do. And besides, I reasoned, as a foreign correspondent and journalist living for the past twenty-five years in Asia and Europe and all around the United States, I've spent much of my life "out" and I was glad to be at a point in my life when I could be home, working.

The second symptom of my codependency, according to my friend, was that my children were still very much on my mind. I was, I thought, helping them through difficult times. But from the perspective of one identification of codependent behavior I was a "caretaker"—a role I had learned to play as the oldest child of an alcoholic mother.

I knew that I was frustrated and felt that I had a responsibility to do what I could for my children and that I wasn't happy about their behavior at the moment. I had been observing to my children for several years that they would do better watching soap opera on television or getting roles on *All My Children* than they would living their drama at tremendous cost to their lives and mine. But I viewed our family situation not as codependency but rather as human life in the last half of the twentieth century .

My friend also pointed out that I was in a bad contractual business situation where I wasn't being represented properly and that my work was not being valued as it should be— another indication to her of destructive codependent behavior.

I began to think that codependent behavior was in the eye of the beholder, but I knew I didn't know enough about codependency to reject its perspective out of hand and so I listened to what she had to say.

What I heard is that codependency is a crippling emotional, mental, and physical disease with dozens and dozens of symptoms. Tens of millions of people suffer from this disease. It is more contagious than AIDS. Codependency can strike anyone who is exposed to an addictive person or thought process. It is transmitted through blood ties, through institutions, the media—through every avenue of our lives. The disease affects the whole person—the emotions, the mind and the body. Causes of the disease are identified as alcohol, drugs, heredity, environment, much of present theology, political double talk and the threat of imminent nuclear war. Family, church, school and government are all identified as breeding grounds of the disease.

Codependent is a word used to describe a person or a state of mind comfortable with artifice and delusion, denial and the repression of individuality. Codependency is not only a buzzword—it is a way of looking at things, a way of examining anger, denial, loss of boundaries of the self and of the nation and its institutions—political, economic and religious.

I heard that one of the symptoms of codependency was a feeling of shame and a consequent poisoned self-consciousness about one's physical and social self. I heard that anyone exposed to repeated lies, anyone who participates in a cover-up of the truth, anyone who can't face simple facts is likely to become codependent.

The only good news for sufferers was regular attendance at one of the Twelve Step programs of Alcoholics Anonymous and/or treatment by a specialist in the field.

My friend was zealous in her insistence that I go to a meeting of the Adult Children of Alcoholics and, as I had asked her to go to church with me when she told me she was interested in God, I felt it was an appropriate exchange of interests and information.

So on a Wednesday evening one spring I found myself at a meeting of the Adult Children of Alcoholics with fifty other people in the basement of an Episcopalian church in New York City.

The meeting had already started when we slipped in and took the only two empty chairs in the room. "I am so mad," a woman was saying. "This day is the first anniversary of my husband's death. I'm mad that he died. I am also grateful for these meetings. I don't think I would have made it through the year if it weren't for ACoA. I'm mad too at my parents for what they did to me," and so she continued with her particulars of life in a dysfunctional family.

Each person who spoke up at this meeting exhibited the same directness, the same depth of gratitude for the help received in their search for freedom from the nightmare of a dysfunctional family.

I was overwhelmed by the brutal honesty, the frank

exposure of emotions, the sincerity of the people at the meeting. Desperate and grateful, with stories of bitterness, the men and women expressed themselves with no attempt to mask rage.

I heard many stories that night. They were stories about human life today and they made soap opera look like insincere child's play. One woman said she had been repeatedly raped by her father. A man said that he and his girlfriend were fighting because it was his father's birthday and he suspected that memories of his alcoholic father were tormenting him. Another woman said she had called a man she had ended a relationship with and had him come over to her place and sleep with her. When he left and said nothing she felt humiliated and hurt and as she told her story she was crying out, "Is it too much to want to be loved?" It was a dramatic evening.

I couldn't catch my breath or talk much at all for several days after the meeting in the church basement. I felt as if I had been hit in the stomach, that my breath was caught in my throat. I recognized that the issues raised had a physical impact on me, and that meant that I better start thinking seriously about codependency and what it might have to do with me.

I have never been a member of a consciousness-raising group. I had never before attended a Twelve Step meeting and it reminded me of a Quaker meeting or of an inspired congregational worship service. It was democratic, the mood was tolerant, the animating purpose of the meeting was healing. It reminded me of the description of the early church in the first years after the Resurrection of Jesus; it felt as I have always imagined the Israelites must have felt just after they passed through the Red Sea to dry land.

But the raw power that I felt in this ACoA meeting was different than any feeling that I have ever had in a traditional church service. There were no musical instruments to join the chorus of glad appreciation for the God of Abraham, Isaac, and Jacob, but there was a spirit of deliverance and gratitude in the air. I was struck by the possibility that this meeting was a present-day application of Jesus' words in the book of Matthew, "For where two or three are gathered together in my name there am I in the midst of them" (18:20). I wondered why this meeting was not upstairs in the sanctuary on Sunday morning, but down here in the basement on a Wednesday night. It was, it seemed to me, church with no fancy clothes, no pretensions, no airs. It was an underground church meeting in the most literal sense.

The Higher Power, God, was the ultimate source of protection, relief, comfort and direction for people attending Twelve Step meetings. But I found that many people whose focus was the management of addiction and codependency problems were struggling with the Third Step of the Twelve Steps—understanding God. They were struggling with their past experience with God and were looking for new and practical definitions of God.

I have never been much of a group person but after my first ACoA meetings I could see why millions attended AA meetings. Everyone took their turn, anyone could speak and be listened to, a sense of understanding of each other's problems filled the air. I saw AA meetings as sanctuaries for hurt and confused human beings—a place where anything can be said with no fear of contradiction. There is no mother or father to say that children should be seen and not heard. There is no lover, husband, wife, or significant other to revise the story being told. There is no authority figure. There are only people who share the same problems and who support and inform each other's insights.

I learned that the prescription for the disease of codependency is found in the Twelve Steps of AA and in the Lord's Prayer. The process of recognizing the symptoms, admission of powerlessness over them, absolute reliance on a Higher Power, forgiveness and sharing the good news of this process with the community are common to them both.

Identifying their codependency is a relief for some people. It brings men and women the understanding that they are not the only ones who feel crazy and angry. They find that they are not the only ones who repeat unhealthy patterns. It reminds them that they need community and support and a place to air their fears and concerns in safety. It reminds them that concern for the healing of the self bridges the otherwise riveting gaps of politics, religion and education.

I spent hours and days reading and trying to understand the literature that I picked up at the ACoA meeting. It was not easy going. It was similar to the experience of moving to a foreign country. It wasn't just the landscape that looked different. The language was different. There were lists of symptoms of codependency and lists of the current vocabulary of words used. There was a new dialect to be learned. I added the words "enabler" and "caretaker" and "codependent" to my vocabulary. An "enabler" was someone who made it possible for someone else to be or to remain an addict.

Where before I had thought a caretaker was someone who worked the grounds of an estate or was perhaps a nurse or guardian, I learned that in the language of codependency a caretaker was a person who felt s/he had to meddle in other people's affairs and control them.

I had always thought that the word "boundary" had to do with real estate, as in "the boundaries of our property," "the boundaries of our nation." I had, of course, thought of the boundaries of imagination and the boundaries of behavior, but I learned in the field of codependency that "crossed boundaries" were incursions by another person into the realm of the individual, and that "setting boundaries" was essential to the reclaiming of the territory of the independent ego. I learned that the language was about the self.

Where politics and business use focus groups to determine which of several issues will engage the voter in each of us, the consumer in each of us, AA Twelve Step meetings serve as a focus group for the wounded and addicted self. They address, without contradiction, the issues of the inconsistencies of our times in the most popular language in the West— the language of the personal self.

It has become almost unpatriotic in some circles not to be codependent. It reminds me of the pointed finger of a bearded Uncle Sam representing the United States on the World War II poster. "Uncle Sam wants you," says the poster. It's hard not to join up.

I also found that some experts in the field of codependency had a following of codependents and a vested interest in the subject just as doctors, lawyers, politicians, psychotherapists, insurance agents and clergy have a vested interest in their fields. I realized that there was more to codependency than meets the eye. A still, small voice told me that we are all codependent and that I should learn more about the terrain of this disease which is endemic to contemporary humanity.

I listened to therapists involved with codependent issues insist with vehemence that years of therapy and meetings were requisite for treatment of the issue. I heard them say that any approach to healing codependency other than theirs was a denial of codependency. I observed that some of them were reluctant to actually turn their lives, or the lives of those they came in contact with, over to God as an immediate source of help. Some of the experts, in a contradiction of the same Twelve Steps that they were using in therapy sessions, said that a dependence on God was another form of addictive, codependent behavior. And that healing could come only through one approach, their approach. I was reminded that codependency is everywhere.

I was reminded that, as in any new movement or idea, there is a period of flashing enthusiasm and healing. Then follows a period of institutionalization, codification and the subsequent rise of a sense of priesthood and authority. With the installation of a priesthood, equality and inspiration often fade. Spontaneity is covered over in perpetual self-examination. Confidence is lost and all things become black or white. One is either in or out of the movement. There are no shades of grey. A sense of fear sets in. Individual self-reliance is denied.

These periods of codification are troubled and paradoxical times for those to whom freshness and vision and self-discovery are imperatives. I live in paradoxical and troubled times, in paradoxical and troubled situations, and so I started reflecting upon my life in the light of codependency. I could see that many of the feelings that I had about myself and my relationships fell squarely into what could be defined as codependency or codependent behavior. I thought about the issues raised by codependents and examined myself and categorized, as best as I could, how much or little of my behavior could be fairly classified as codependent.

I began to focus all my attention, study and prayer on what, in my life, I presently understood to be codependent behavior. I looked at my relationship to my family, my church, my sense of God, my work, my friends and made lists of specific relationships and behavior that could be classified as codependent.

I studied and read the ten most popular books in the

country on the subject of codependency and read the Big Book of Alcoholics Anonymous and researched the history of AA. I spent a year in interviews and meetings and discussions with hundreds and hundreds of people involved at all levels and stages of the codependency issue. The issue of codependency is so large, so broad and so deep that in that year, even with all that effort and study, I realized that I had probably developed only a nodding acquaintance with the symptoms and language of the disease currently named codependency.

Naming a disease in order to heal it is effective. Naming is power. I realized that naming behavior as codependent was a blessing. It gave me a sense of how important it was to deal directly and specifically with any disease. If I know that I am sick, I reasoned, then I can get well. If I don't know that I am sick, if I think sick is well, I will think that feeling bad is an inevitable consequence of heredity, environment, of biology or chemistry, of sin. I do not like feeling bad, I don't like victimization, I don't like domination, I did not want to be a co-conspirator in pain, suffering, or powerlessness.

I drove my family slightly crazy with the examination of our behavior in the light of codependency. I talked about it to fellow church members and asked them to examine with me our sense of church and God in the light of codependency. I talked to friends in and out of Twelve Step meetings about codependency. I attended all kinds of Twelve Step meetings in several parts of the United States and I read all the literature two or three times.

I spent a year applying my understanding of God to the specific problem of the disease of codependency. In AA terms I spent a year "working the program." In biblical terms, I spent a year separating the tares of codependency from the wheat of spiritual self-reliance.

I found that the Bible was the single most instructive book available on the recognition and healing of codependency. The Bible contains messages for codependents, stories about other codependents, prayers for codependents, answers for codependents and addicts. I turned to the Bible, where the Lord's Prayer is recorded, to help me with codependency and its effects on my life—to find how to heal codependency.

The Bible contains all the elements of the Twelve Steps. It illustrates forgiveness in human affairs. It says that codependency is crippling and paralytic. It says that codependency is not the will of God, not unmanageable. Its words say that codependency was healed, can be healed, must be healed, will be healed.

I've studied the Bible in and out of organized church for twenty-five years—in graduate school, with groups, with various teachers and by myself. And for five years, I wrote a newspaper column about the effects of biblical interpretation on women and society, on politics and religion. Many of those columns were about how some present theology causes codependency.

I don't pretend to know everything that there is to know about codependency. No one knows all about the subject which continues to mushroom and is now, in sheer numbers, the nations' leading disease. And I certainly don't pretend to know everything there is to know about the Bible.

I've spent years in the desert where there was no organized church and years in Southeast Asian countries where there were few, if any, Christian or Jewish services. My need for church or worship or God did not disappear in those places. But as traditional church was almost non-existent in most of Southeast Asia, I had to rely for spiritual instruction on the Word of the Bible for worship, instruction, church and a link with my history and culture.

I learned much in these periods that I would not have learned in my neighborhood church. With no priest or minister there to stand in for me at the altar, I learned, among other things, to translate the communion service into a spiritual event without bread or wine. I learned to interpret the Word of the Bible as daily messages from God, as reflections on politics and social behavior in a patriarchy. I learned to view its voice as that of a friend. I learned to rely on the very presence of God as I understood the God described in the Bible. Over and over again I learned the value of spiritual self-reliance. In physical and emotional danger I turned to God and found "a very present help in trouble." I learned the value of radical dependence on God.

It would take more than the pages of this book to list the different symptoms and recount examples and experiences that illustrate codependency in the world. It would take more than the pages of this book to recount examples that I feel are evidence of God's presence and help in dealing with codependency.

After a year studying codependency and applying my understanding of the Higher Power to the issue, I realized that the study of codependent behavior in the Bible would be meat for more than one book, that sermons could be preached on codependency and spiritual sense, that threaded through the Bible is the theme of finding spiritual self-reliance.

At the end of the year, after studying and listening and learning what I could about codependency, after a year of relating the Twelve Steps of AA to research on the Bible in the light of codependency, I found that my family relationships were better. I found that I had increased my understanding of God. I found that I still liked to stay home and that my work situation still frustrated me and that if I wanted to break my contract I probably could but the lawyers weren't convinced that it would be easy or even possible.

Recognition of codependency caused me to see the "curse" of codependency as a blessing which renews the sense of the sacredness of each individual self and its relation to the Higher Power, God. Recognizing codependency is no fun but it does lead to a better understanding of God and to the joy and clarity found in government by a Higher Power.

For countless millions, understanding the Higher Power and discovering spiritual self-reliance is a process which they began by recognizing codependency.

2

Some Who, What, When, Where and Whys of Codependency

One of the most poignant and extreme examples of codependency in current history occurred when over nine hundred people who had become codependent to Jim Jones' addictions died when they poisoned themselves with cyanide at Jonestown in the Guyanese jungle.

Most codependency is not seen as graphically. But it exists, nevertheless, as a widespread condition in private homes, one-on-one, or family by family. In the broadest terms, codependency exists wherever there is exposure to addictive habits which, if relinquished, cause severe trauma.

As a result, food, sex, television, church, politics, the workplace, relationships of all kinds are arenas in which addiction and codependency exist. And, as the emphasis on growth of the individual self has become a major influence in western public consciousness, the term *codependent* has been used in books and lectures, on television shows and in the daily conversation of many of the people in this country to describe not just those related to alcohol and drug addicts but *anyone* dependent on or responding to any addiction.

All of society is addicted, according to Anne Wilson Schaef, a pioneer in the field of codependency and the author of *When Society Becomes an Addict*. And if all of society is addicted, then by definition, all of society is codependent.

Specifically, codependents are people related to addicts or to addictive thought and behavior patterns. Codependency becomes multi-generational when children of addicts experience addictive behavior as if it were normal and rational, and adopt it as their own. Codependents are people who suffer because someone else in their family or home was captive to addiction.

Addiction is no respecter of persons. Addiction comes in many forms. The increase alone of chemical substance abuse in the United States has caused an increase in the number of codependents in the nation. U.S. government statistics say that there are twenty-four million drinking alcoholics in the country. There are six million children under the age of eighteen who live in homes with alcoholic parents. Alcohol afflicts more children than any physical disease and studies that show the impact of codependency on physical ills have only just begun.

By definition, codependents include the men, women, children, people of all political persuasions, religious denominations and skin color, who are related to those twenty-four million alcoholics. No one political party, no one denomination, no one racial group has a monopoly on addiction among its members.

One expert says that codependency is:

> an emotional, psychological, and behavioral condition that develops as a result of an individual's prolonged exposure to, and practice of, a set of oppressive rules— rules which prevent the open expression of feeling as well as the direct discussion of personal and interpersonal problems. (Robert Subby, *Co-Dependence: An*

Emerging Issue [Pomano Beach, Fla.: Health Communications, 1984], p. 126)

Another says:

Sometimes, codependent behavior becomes inextricably entangled with being a good wife, mother, husband, brother, or Christian. (Melody Beattie, *Codependent No More* [New York: Harper/Hazelden, 1987], p. 22)

Expanding definitions of codependency include people who do not have satisfying relationships. Codependents are people from dysfunctional families of all sorts.

According to the experts, there are, at minimum, fifty million men, women and children now in the nation who have lived in alcoholic homes. Those people, according to the experts, view the world of relationships, politics, and religion through the lens of codependency.

There are many books and articles on the subject of codependency and a long list of the symptoms and behavioral responses of codependents.

The single best way that I know to discover the nature of codependency is to attend a meeting of self-described codependents. At Al-Anon or Adult Children of Alcoholics or Alateen meetings you will hear men and women and children describe their lives with addiction. You will hear them talk about their behavior and their feelings and you will find stack upon stack of printed materials which describe symptoms, characteristics, behavior patterns, labels for the behaviors of codependency. You will be astonished and moved.

If you haven't yet attended a meeting, the best synthesis of the features of codependency that I have come across in my

research is by Michael J. Bader. Writing in *Tikkun*, Bader, a
psychotherapist and director of the graduate psychology
program at New College of California says:

> The family system that generates the pathological behav-
> ior, the relationship addiction and the masochism [in-
> volved in *Women Who Love Too Much* or the Adult Child
> of the Alcoholic] is depicted by this literature in a surpris-
> ingly uniform fashion. Its salient features may be sum-
> marized as follows:
>
> 1. Dysfunctional families are those in which the par-
> ents don't provide the child with love, nurturance, and re-
> spect. These parents are not healthy enough to be good
> role models for the child, nor can they fulfill their roles
> as caregivers or as happy marital partners. They are
> psychologically disabled, usually by addictions of some
> kind or by other forms of mental illness, and they make
> unpredictable and narcissistic use of the child, who con-
> sequently feels neglected or abused. The parents deny
> various aspects of reality: Most important, they deny
> their own addiction, and they invalidate the child's
> accurate perceptions about that addiction.
>
> 2. The child becomes the caregiver in the family,
> either because s/he is identified as such by the parents or
> because the parents are just too disabled to be able to care
> for themselves or others. The child mothers the mother
> and/or the father and comes to accept guilt and responsi-
> bility for the family's problems.
>
> 3. The child mistakes being needed for being loved.
> Moreover, since s/he can never quite solve the family's
> problems, her or his underlying feelings of being un-
> loved and worthless only intensify. The child then

redoubles the efforts to secure love by giving 'until it hurts,' which escalates the entire process.

4. The child's attempts to 'cure' the parents through self-sacrifice, though never successful, are continually elicited by the parents' inappropriate dependence on the child and by the child's underlying need for affirmation. The child gets 'hooked' into a no-win situation.

5. These patterns continue into adulthood. People repeat what they experienced as children because it is 'familiar,' or because, now that they are adults, they want to make it come out right. In other words, repetition is often an attempt at mastery.

6. Specifically, this repetition means that people raised in this kind of family system choose partners and relationships in which their own needs are subordinated to the needs of others, in which they again play the role of the overly responsible caretaker or parent.

7. In repeating their childhood dramas, people once again mistake being needed for being loved and desperately try to change their defective partners into the men or women of their childhood dreams. These attempts, of course, are of no avail and only deepen these people's depression and self-hatred. Their adult relationships, therefore, are exactly like addictions—they use them to escape from depression, but these relationships simply aggravate the original symptoms.

8. These adults are inordinately hard on themselves, self-punitive, and often driven, because they believe that their misery and self-sacrifice will be rewarded with love and approval and will make up for the faults and deficiencies of their loved ones.

9. Many of these adults become alcoholics or sub-

stance abusers because of a combination of heredity, imitation and/or an intense need for relief from anxiety and depression. They then begin this process anew when they start their own families. (Michael J. Bader, "Looking for Addictions in All the Wrong Places," *Tikkun* 3, no. 6 [November-December 1988] 13)

The study, identification and means of recovering from codependent behavior has become a modern behavioral science complete with pioneers, gurus, leading thinkers and generally interested parties. Some experts see codependency everywhere and in everyone and these experts and their followers redefine behavior in the light of their definitions of codependency.

I actually met a man in an airport recently who, when he offered to help with my one bag while he carried three, explained this obviously foolish behavior by introducing himself in the language of codependent behavior as a "caretaker." In other times he would have been called a frustrated gentleman wanting to help a lady. Now he saw himself as codependent.

Codependency is turning the traditions and values of society upside down.

Codependency is in the atmosphere of popular thought. Its language fills the air. Codependents begin to recognize themselves in the lyrics of popular songs. The airwaves spill out messages of codependence minute by minute in songs such as "You're Nobody Till Somebody Loves You." Willie Nelson sings about a good-hearted woman in love with a two-timing man—who loves him in spite of his wicked ways which she doesn't understand, and about a woman that he didn't treat well but who was always on his mind.

Another popular song says, "every heartbreak and temptation only makes me love you more." And one current song recognizes the market; its words mirror descriptions of addicted and codependent behavior—a woman knows she's in a real bad situation and nevertheless sits by the phone waiting for it to ring so that she can talk to a man who doesn't need her the way she needs him. The lyrics go on to describe the resulting paralysis, confusion, and despair involved in addiction and codependency.

Addiction and codependency are in the air and all over the airwaves. Denial of spiritual self-reliance is the theme of the day. The code words of codependency are legion. What used to be called the proper role in family life is now called "caretaking, enabling, lost child syndrome."

The language of codependency is also laced with political and religious language. It is as if, subconsciously, codependents realize that there is more to codependency than what went on in the home.

Symptoms of codependency in political language are called "loss of boundaries," "safety," "protection," "information," and "rights." The healing or management of codependency is pursued in religious terms—God, "Higher Power," "trust," "forgiveness," "gratitude."

The symptoms of codependency can be viewed from many perspectives. They can be viewed as yet another sociological phenomenon of a troubled nation, as the direct result of addictions and lies and false priorities, as a call to spiritual growth, as the psyche's scream for spirituality in daily life.

All of that said it is not, however, in the language of politics or religion or the nation that codependency hits home. It is the recognition that codependent addiction is not about *them,* or *him,* or *her*; but about the *I* that sets the codependent on the path of change.

It is the recognition that *I* am the one who is upset, who talks all the time about *my* mate or *my* child or *my* boss or *my* church or *my* group. *I* am the one who can't listen to anyone else. *I* am the one who can't work or live or think of anything else but the problem.

Codependents take impersonal things personally. "I've got no trouble with alcohol but with the '*-ism—I, self, me*'," said a woman at one Twelve Step meeting I attended. "I can walk by something three times and I'm an addict. No wonder I'm tired all the time. I'm fighting battles all night in my sleep."

How do you know if you are codependent?

If you have been raised in a dysfunctional family, then you are, experts say, most probably codependent. And, many of them add, if you don't think that you are codependent then you probably are. But what if you think your family was just fine? Or what if you've never questioned your family behavior but just accepted the way things were?

Following are some questions that people have asked themselves in order to determine if they are codependent.

Am I compulsive?

Do I believe I can take care of myself—emotionally, economically, spiritually?

Am I a doormat? Do I let people walk all over me? Say yes when I mean no, or yes when I mean maybe, or "I don't know"?

Do I have a public face and a private face?

Do I express my honest feelings?

Do I know my honest feelings?

Do I try to control other people's behavior in hopes it will give me strength or identity?

Do I get easily confused?

Do I overeat?

Do I refer to other people or institutions for my identity?

Do I consider myself less a person than the people I deal with?

Do I lie to protect and cover up for people I love?

Do I trust myself, my feelings, my decisions?

Am I repeating unfullfilling patterns? Am I stuck and do I seem not to be making progress?

Do I feel abandoned? Worthless?

Do I tire easily for no apparent reason?

Am I afraid of change?

Do I hold onto the past, tell the same stories over and over? Am I afraid of something new and different?

Am I ashamed?

Do I feel I have to be good?

Have I suffered abuse—physical, mental, emotional or spiritual?

Asking themselves these questions and listening honestly to the answers has surprised many people. They discover that if they are honest with themselves they are to some degree codependent.

"Yes, thousands of people really did write letters to the television show Marcus Welby, M.D. asking advice about their medical problems," says a widely quoted magazine article.

"People are confused," says Joel Achenbach whose article is quoted in the *Utne Reader* ("Creeping Surrealism," no. 30, p. 112). "Liberated from such basic responsibilities as the growing of food, the making of clothes, the construction of shelter, people in the late twentieth century have entered into a revolutionary phase of human development in which they passively accept a cartoon version of reality promulgated by the media rather than trusting their own instincts to figure reality out for themselves. From this mess has arisen a strange sort of comfort with artifice and falsehood."

Pure (and undefiled religion) . . . is this, To visit the fatherless and widows in their affliction and to keep (oneself) unspotted from the world. (James 1:27, Authorized [King James] Version [AV])

It is the job, the calling of religion to heal the sick, to care for the women and the children, the poor and the hungry, the abused and the battered among us. It is the function of religion to gather beneath its wings the weary and the comfortless.

We live now in times where theologians talk of a God that is all-good but not all-powerful. Or they talk of a God that is all-powerful but not all-good. This is the game of "who can you trust?" Rather than preach the message of an all-powerful, everpresent God, good, available to widows and children and illustrated in the first chapter of Genesis and throughout the Bible, religion often teaches the sociological and historical backdrop of the Bible as the leading Truth. What is often taught is the background of fear, sin, death, delayed gratification, inscrutable ways and mysteries, along with a hierarchy of

God, then man, then woman, then everything else; and these most often relayed by studied and ordained men.

According to Arnold Toynbee in his book *Christianity Among the Religions of the World* (New York: Scribner's 1957, p. 23), "Hinduism, if I have read it right intuitively seeks to save the absoluteness of God at the cost of His goodness. The Judaic religions intuitively try to save His goodness at the cost of His absoluteness. And neither solution has been a true solution, because for human beings, God has to be both absolute and good, and the two requirements cannot be reconciled in terms of logic."

Since we are all human beings with needs for an all-good power, a loss of this message—in the light of codependency—creates a congregation—a nation—of codependents.

Codependent behavior is identified as a hell that includes shame and denial and a list of other attitudes and feelings which most people feel or have felt in the course of their lifetime. It is identified as negative, destructive and as something that prevents both the codependent and the addict from discovering spiritual self-reliance. Codependent behavior often includes a lack of trust. Codependents, it is argued, cannot trust now because they could not trust in the alcoholic and/or dysfunctional family of their childhood.

Most people who are "working" on their codependency feel like the children of the children of Adam and Eve—they are suffering because of the sin, shame and denial of their parents.

Codependent behavior patterns the curse on Adam and Eve described in the second story of Creation in the Book of Genesis. It includes shame and guilt and suffering for the children as a result of the parents' behavior. A substitution of the words "substance abuse" for the word "fruit" in the text is instructive in understanding how addiction results in code-pendency.

The entire text can be found from Chapter 2, verse 6, "and a mist went up from the earth and watered the whole face of the ground." It includes the seduction of one member of a family, consequent shame, admission, denial, suffering, and domination. It includes sorrow and endless labor and division in the family and a feeling of separation from the abundance of a good God, a Father who supplies His children with all that they need. The story of Adam and Eve is a broad description of the effects of substance abuse as seen through the lens of codependency.

The first story of Creation includes no addictive code-pendency. In Chapter One of Genesis, through the fifth verse of Chapter Two, there is no sorrow, no punishment, nothing that is not a blessing. In the first story of Creation everything is good and every thing works together for good. Male and female are simultaneously created; one does not tempt nor dominate the other. The story is one of heaven and earth and harmony.

The second story of Creation, the story of Adam and Eve, is more familar to us. It is the one we believe more readily, because we see the story in human history and around us every day. We see and hear about wars and rumors of wars, about peoples who believe in One God fighting over interpretations of that God. We see, through the lens of codependency, not the first story of Creation but the second.

More than one denomination claims to be the One True Way. People who do not accept the One True Way are thought to be lost, without the benefit of God. How an individual determines the One True Way in the face of conflicting claims is confusing for many.

How, for example, does one who believes that every

word of Jesus is literally true reconcile the teaching that heaven is someplace one goes after death with Jesus' saying, "The kingdom of heaven is within you" (Luke 17:21, AV)?

From the perspective of codependency, religious codependents are people who lean on the pastor, the priest, the minister to interpret for them, suffer for them, tell them what to do. Those who perpetuate and those who believe and support false doctrine, false theologies are, by definition, engaged in codependent behavior. Codependents, according to the definitions of codependency, are people who faithfully follow ministers that are lying about themselves or to the congregation.

Some therapists in the field of codependency are now treating ministers and priests for codependency. One of these therapists explained to me, "Ministers are caretakers—they have their own codependent issues." Another friend involved in the field said, "Being a caretaker is no reason not to be a minister; in fact it may be a prerequisite."

Those who feel that they have left the issue of God behind them in rational thinking are faced with being addicted to and codependent upon nothing higher than themselves—which has the possibility of being limited in scope. History and common sense show that the doctrine of the self is incomplete and the individual who subscribes to the self as the highest power on the planet often reaches for emotional highs to mask the sense of isolation.

As I began research on this book I discovered that codependency is all around, that it is contagious, something I wanted to warn friends about.

At the same time that I listened to self-defined codependents describe themselves in terms of the biblical description of Adam and Eve I also heard people who did not know much of anything about codependency talking about their problems without having a sense that what they were talking about was classic codependency motivating their behavior.

I had mixed feelings, which codependents would call the arousal of my own codependent issues. I began to think these feelings were similar to the ones Moses must have had when he was told to pick up his rod, saw it become a snake and then a rod again. I had company. I wasn't the only one who learned that things weren't what they seemed.

I could see that I responded to my children's behavior in the way that I had responded to my mother's alcoholic behavior. I hoped things would be all right, I was patient, I was tolerant, I didn't want to cause problems for them. And then I would get really mad at the behavior and go on with my own life. But I wasn't sure whether or not that was a fairly normal process for most people.

I identified my own codependency through not only that feeling I have sometimes that I may have left the stove on, but also feelings of not wanting to deal with difficult family problems. Or how I feel when I listen to Patsy Cline singing "I Fall to Pieces."

I began to wonder if people who defined themselves as codependent were becoming addicted to that definition and view of themselves. And I began to feel, as some of them told me they were, that they were living in a closed-circuit system of codependency. The definition of codependency had become self-fulfilling.

I wanted to warn them to wake up and take a look at this issue and handle it with the dominion promised to the male and female of God's creating in the first chapter of Genesis—the children of Light who were promised dominion over all the earth.

I wanted to see for myself how codependency could be healed.

3

Women Who
Needed Help

Most experts say that the first thing to do about codependency is to recognize it. Melody Beattie says that sometimes codependent behavior becomes inextricably linked with being a good wife, mother, husband, brother or Christian.

I agree with Beattie that sometimes being "good" is codependency but I do not think that it is ever inextricably linked. Good behavior can be separated from codependent behavior. The links can be broken.

I have a friend whose nightmare of codependency and painful separation from it I recently witnessed.

My friend Connie is a totally devout Christian woman whose first husband and father of her four children left her one day three years ago—without notice—for another woman, his secretary. Connie was devastated. She was forty-two with four young teenagers. She had been married since she was nineteen. She had never slept with anyone but her husband, she had never paid a bill, she hadn't worked since the first year of her marriage, she hadn't the faintest idea how to cope with life as a single person; but she thought that the Bible and church would be a great source of comfort and inspiration and guidance in her hour of acute need and desperation. Her father had been a minister and she had loved and respected him and trusted that he was—that the entire church, the entire body of

believers in the nation were—good and would be good to her.
That had been her experience as a married woman.

No one in Connie's family had, for the past three genera-
tions that she knew of, been addicted to alcohol or drugs. The
entire family had been active and totally devoted to church and
to God as they understood Him.

What happened to Connie doesn't seem possible, but I
have heard similar stories from so many women over so many
years that I know it is the fact. The story goes like this.

"People said things to me like, 'You're a lovely woman,
you'll be married again in no time.' And they would say, 'A
woman can't raise teenagers alone. You really need a man in
your life.' A few people said, 'Well, its very hard, the sexual
thing, I mean.' "

"I believed them. I never really investigated for myself
whether I needed a man or whether I could raise my children
alone. I believed them because I believed anything. I didn't
ever investigate any of my beliefs for myself. I'd never been
without my father or a husband and I had no practical experience in operating without a man."

Connie's teenagers were spending some time being
spoiled by their guilty father and his paramour and before she
knew it the plumber who came to fix the sink ended up in my
friend's bed for an afternoon of sex.

She was so ashamed, so guilty, so frightened of her lack
of sexual control that when a man she had met in church a few
years ago called and asked her out she leapt at the chance for
the date. The man told her he had always had a crush on her,
that his wife had left him with three teenage boys and that he
had always idealized my friend and wanted to marry her.

What's a poor girl to do ? Here was a way out—a church
member, a needy father, a larger family. Her former husband

had never been to church with her. This looked like a blessing from the Lord for sure. Single men in church are pursued and here she was being pursued. She went to bed with this man, thought husbands were husbands, some better than others at money or sex or parenting, and she called a few friends to ask them what they thought about this new man's marriage proposal.

I told her that it is possible to live without being married. That in fact to some it is preferable—and she said, "I wanted to hear that," and she hung up and the man came to the door with flowers and a ring and some desperate flattery and she married him.

Two weeks after the marriage she found letters in the dresser from a woman that he was (as recently as two days earlier, according to the postmark on the letter) sleeping with. The woman was threatening to kill herself.

It took six months for my friend to realize that her new husband was a closet drinker, a lousy father and a chronic adulterer. She had been looking at him through the eyes of a good girl, a trusting, guilty believer. It took two years to get the divorce, and all in all, my friend figures that it cost her $150,000 by the time she moved to his home, fixed it up, left his home, moved back to hers and changed her children's schools three times.

"It never felt like home to me at his house," Connie said. "And I didn't and really still don't know what a husband is all about, why I didn't listen to myself, or trust that I would be taken care of directly by God. But I did—I do—know what home feels like. I've decided to start at my home, here with my kids and my life and not worry about a husband. God is my husband. But I don't know why my church didn't tell me that. I was codependent on the belief of Adam and Eve. I believed

that woman came out of man. I didn't believe the first promise
of Creation—that man and woman were created simultaneously and equal. I believed a myth and not the reality."

It took my friend some time to get the divorce. The day
she did she felt better. It was not just a flush of relief that she
felt. It was the recognition of her own spiritual identity as a
person and as a woman—a powerful woman.

She is dealing maturely and honestly with her first
husband. She is full of joy about her children and able to cope
with all that having four teenagers involves. She has a busy
career and many men courting her. Connie has a fresh
perspective on church that is based on equality of the sexes. It
is blessing hundreds of people in the remarkable work she is
doing praying with people who are drawn to her because of her
love and compassion and new-found experience.

Laura was taking care of a sick friend from church and it
turned out that the sick friend was sick because she was
pregnant with not her husband's, but another man's child. The
husband, also a member of the same church, turned more and
more to Laura who was nursing his wife.

He, after all, was broken hearted and important and had
to work and so gave the two children they already had to Laura
for what he said was two weeks. Six months later Laura, who
had two children of her own, still had his children and she told
their mutual minister that she was concerned the husband's
attentions were becoming directed toward her, and that even
though he and his wife were now getting divorced she didn't
feel at all comfortable.

Laura had lived most of her early life in the wake of the
effects of her mother's alcoholism. She was the caretaker in
the family and she had been glad to find religion for herself

when she was in her early 20's. She trusted her minister—the father figure that she hadn't had at home since her parents' divorce when she was three.

The minister told her that the man was important. That his work should be considered. And, the minister added, there are those children to raise. It was, he told Laura, really her job as a Christian woman to submit to what was obviously the Lord's will. "And besides," he added, "you are a very attractive and disconcerting woman, and unmarried, you are causing too many people a problem." Laura felt shame and responsibility and she listened to the minister with faithful devotion.

The man and the minister had a meeting and several couples in the church were called in, and before she knew it Laura was crying and begging to be released from this, by now, impending marriage. The husband-to-be and the minister consoled her by assuring her that they knew what was best for her and would take care of her and provide for her material and spiritual and emotional needs. Laura loved God more than anything and she thought that the minister spoke for God, so she did what he said as her heart sank.

"They didn't take care of me," says Laura. "I tried to get an annulment on my wedding day. Before I had ever slept with him he started talking about his first wife and his sexual problems and started ranting and raving about women and how deceitful they were. He called the minister from the restaurant we were in after the ceremony and he put me on the phone with our minister, who told me I was evil and that he would pray for me to be a good wife." Laura backed down.

A year later Laura found her husband in the closet reading *Playboy* magazines and she began to put together possible reasons why his first wife committed adultery. The only way Laura could break free was to announce that she was about to commit adultery, ask for a divorce, commit adultery the next day and set about reconstructing her life and the lives of her children. Both Laura and her husband were victims of codependency based on men's fear of being alone and women's fear of not somehow doing the right thing—abandonment and guilt.

Laura moved and changed churches, but it was years before either she or her ex-husband really recovered. And years before they could learn to trust again.

These are only two of the horror stories of codependent churchmen and -women. Of course you don't have to go to church to be codependent and choose the wrong man or woman, and you aren't necessarily codependent if you go to church and marry someone you met there. Many women and men tell stories of meeting partners in church and marrying them and living happily ever after, more or less. But women and men in church are susceptible to codependency, as it is currently defined, because much of the information available to them comes from people who had things other than the spiritually equal rights of women on their minds.

I discovered this fact and its enforcer—intimidation—for myself at about the same time I discovered that I was religiously codependent. I was being a good girl and going to a two-week class given by a minister who had a terrific grasp of the poetry of the cosmos.

The course was on what the Bible has to do with our lives and the minister-teacher, a learned and experienced man of his church said, "Here is a hypothetical case. How would you pray about this? The husband is beating the wife and her life is hell. How can we change her beliefs through prayer?"

There was silence as the group turned to their papers and pencils to write prayers to change the hypothetical woman's belief.

I raised my hand.

"The first thing," I said, "is to get her out of there. And then what about his beliefs?"

There was more silence.

If the woman was in a burning house, I thought, I'd get her out of there before I worried about changing her beliefs about fire or houses.

"Well," the teacher said, "yes, I suppose so."

'I suppose so?'

Sixteen of the twenty women in the group assumed that if a husband was beating his wife there must be something wrong with the wife that needed changing. Only four women thought there was something wrong with the reasoning behind the teacher's question.

Talk about codependency! It's to weep over.

I have a broken heart when women sit silently and accept a portrait of themselves as responsible for someone else's problem. I want to say, "wake up! It's the twentieth century. Women are not responsible for a man's thinking. Women can think for themselves. So can men. Women can ask questions, they are not afraid of the 'terror that flies by night.' Women are spiritual ideas of God, too. Women are not the cause of arguments. Domination is the cause of arguments."

I wanted to say, "Love yourselves, girls. Get with the program. This codependency has got to go."

I thought to myself, You mean am I supposed to believe this guy? I know that it is wrong to go into someone's mind and mess with what they think. I know that things aren't what they seem but you've got to draw the line somewhere. And that "somewhere" is physical abuse. Don't waffle on this one. It's the man who's hitting. Even if I'm wrong and she is wrong, for God's sake be merciful and get her out of there so she can repent in safety and security in a women's shelter.

I heard my own reaction to this minister. I could not believe that I was as convinced as I was that the way to stop something is to stop it. I could not believe that I had spent years in flattering adoration of men who believed that the story of Adam and Eve was the literal and psychological truth.

I realized that I had spent years as a codependent woman by thinking that I had done something wrong. I was codependent on Eve.

The moment when I really recognized the depth of my own religious codependency was when I called another minister friend of mine and was moaning and groaning to him about the level of thought of the class and he said to me, "Well, now you know, God is your only teacher."

This was an epiphanic moment for me, a rush that swept through my body and lit up my face and enlightened my eyes and said, *right*. It was the Comforter, Spirit, bringing all things to my remembrance. *Right,* God is my only teacher.

When I recognized the import of that statement I stopped some of my subtle dependence on others in church. I had been relying on others to teach me and to answer thorny questions for me and I began to discover that what I longed for was spiritual self-reliance.

I began to discover that I actually possessed spiritual self-reliance and had been covering some of it up because I didn't feel that I could possibly know as much as some of the men I felt had more experience. I didn't believe as much in inspiration as I did in the priesthood. And I was the loser for it.

In the course of writing a newspaper column on women

and religion I found many examples of women who were concerned about the issue of codependency in the church— although codependency was not the name they used to describe the condition. One was brought to my attention inadvertently.

"You'll love this," my friend said on the phone. "A group of Christian women here are meeting regularly using the Bible to help them lose weight."

My friend knew of my interest in people using the Bible not as abstract theology but as a practical guide for today's problems. I think there are great uncharted fields of study in the Bible and am always anxious to hear about people studying the original texts for today's problems. So I went to the west coast to visit the women who, I thought, were exploring the Bible in order to discover what it had to say about appetites, food, individuality, spiritual weight. What I found was something else.

As I looked around the basement room of the church I could see dozens and dozens of women who did not, I thought, qualify as being "fat." They may not have been a size six and they may have felt that they would like to lose ten pounds or so, but only three of the women in the room looked as if their weight was something they needed extra help to control.

I don't know how many of these women were raised in addictive homes, but as I listened to them share their feelings with each other I was struck by the very clear impression that what they suffered from was not an eating disorder but codependency and domination. "I want to eat soup and salad for dinner," one woman said, "but Charlie, my husband, insists that I eat steak and potatoes and bread just like he does. And he makes the kids eat what he wants to also."

"I know what you mean," said another, "Harry took us to

Howard Johnson's for dinner the other night and I wanted just some soup, but he made me eat fried chicken and mashed potatoes and later I was really sick." "I don't have time to do my Bible study and take care of two small kids," said another woman. "I eat on the run and if it weren't for this class I wouldn't get to the Bible during the week. I've asked Dick to watch the kids at night or for a few hours on the weekend so that I could go for a walk or study quietly, but he says the children are my job—at least at this age."

It was at this point that the leader of the group turned to Paul's writings and said, "Here is a quotation that will help you to meet the demands on your life, to stop eating so much and to deal with your overloaded work schedule," and she turned to Philippians, chapter 4, verse 13 and quoted Paul, " I can do all things through Christ which strengtheneth me." What she was doing was using that text to support the idea of losing weight. It didn't occur to her that the text could be used to have the strength to say no to a husband's dictatorial sense of food consumption. "I can do all things (including say no) through Christ which strengtheneth me."

The Amplified Bible on Philippians 4:13 says, "I have strength for all things in Christ Who empowers me—I am ready for anything and equal to anything through Him Who infuses inner strength into me (that is, I am self-sufficient in Christ's sufficiency)" (Grand Rapids, Mich.: Zondervan, 1965, p. 309).

Another Bible verse was chosen and read in a context which assumed that what was needed here was more strength to put up with what the women's own instincts told them was oppressive. It wasn't the women's desire to eat that was causing them to look at themselves as overweight and not stylishly attractive. Their desire to eat what their bodies and minds and spirits told them to eat was being subjugated. They were intimidated by their husbands who were using food to assert superiority over them.

Obviously these sincere Christian women were denying their own feelings, denying that God knows each individual's needs as a woman, as a person. Not one of them could imagine a husband saying, "Well, of course darling, your body knows what's good for it and I love you for knowing yourself."

Not one of them could imagine saying to her husband, "God is telling me what to eat and I'm at peace about my own food intake. And by the way, I hope it won't be an inconvenience to you, but I'll be gone Saturday afternoon from 2–6. You'll love playing with the kids and getting them down for their nap. I'm going swimming and then I'll decide what else to do with my time as I listen to God."

The Bible, which millions and millions of women read, is full of stories of codependents—men and women. It is also full of stories of God-dependent people and of codependency healed.

Your own research will show these stories to you as you understand the nature of codependency as contrasted to spiritual self-reliance. One of the many stories in the Bible about codependency is the story of Salome and John the Baptist. When the king promised Salome anything in the world that she asked for in exchange for her dance, Salome asked her mother what to ask for. The head of the Baptist was what momma wanted—and what she got from her codependent daughter.

There is a story in the Gospel of John of another classic codependent.

"Now there is at Jerusalem by the sheep market a pool, which is called in the Hebrew tongue Bethesda, having five porches. In these lay a great multitude of impotent folk, of blind, halt, withered, waiting for the moving of the water. For an angel went down at a certain season into the pool, and troubled the water: whoseover then first after the troubling of the water stepped in was made whole of whatsoever disease he had. And a certain man was there, which had an infirmity thirty and eight years. When Jesus saw him lie, and knew that he had been now a long time in that case, he saith unto him, Wilt thou be made whole? The impotent man answered him, Sir, I have no man, when the water is troubled, to put me into the pool: but while I am coming, another steppeth down before me. Jesus saith unto him, Rise, take up thy bed, and walk. And immediately the man was made whole, and took up his bed, and walked . . ." (John 5:2–9, AV).

The five porches of the pool at Bethesda can be seen to symbolize the five senses—those senses that make our impotence, our paralyzed movements, our codependency seem so real. We wait, because of our limited senses, for someone else to help us. In chronic codependency we wait for someone else to build our thoughts, approve of our motives, provide our dwelling place.

Like the man by the pool, we wait for help when all we have to do is to rise and walk ourselves.

Codependency is debilitating. It results in sickness, abnormal behavior, repeated failure, unsatisfied longings. It is the opposite of a healthy, balanced spiritual life.

What that slavish codependency does is block the individual from finding the self and from living out the wholesome and healthy desires of that self in a spirit of freedom while it waits for someone else to help.

Codependency prevents one from seeing the broad panorama of good that is spread before the eyes like a feast set on the evening of the last Day of Creation—the Creation described in Genesis 1. The spiritual cost of codependency is a loss of an individual, conscious, loved and loving relationship to the self and to God.

Codependency is not a peaceful, close relationship to a vital, living, practical, everpresent God—but God dependency is.

4

GodDependency as Spiritual Self-Reliance

God dependency is based on the premise that God is all-good and all-powerful and that each individual is free, regardless of parents' addictions, to recognize, understand and put into practice that goodness and power for him or herself. A basic tenet of God dependency is that each individual, regardless of past or present circumstance, may turn to God and find help and freedom. This idea that each person has a direct and accountable relationship to God is still a radical thought in some circles. But its basis in Judeo-Christian thought is thousands of years old.

Women and men who are God dependent are encouraged and comforted by the principle of personal responsibility as stated in Ezekiel: "What mean ye, that ye use this proverb concerning the land of Israel, saying, The fathers have eaten sour grapes, and the children's teeth are set on edge? As I live, saith the Lord God, ye shall not have occasion any more to use this proverb in Israel. Behold, all souls are mine" (Ezek. 18:2–4, AV).

The text that follows separates the actions of parent and child from each other and roots an individual's relationship to God, and not in the visitation of the sins of the fathers upon the sons. The sins of the fathers are the sins of the fathers and not of the sons. This idea was radical, prophetic theology at that time, and to some degree it still is. The perspective of an individual relationship to God replaces dependence on family with dependence on God, Life.

God dependency replaces the symptoms of codependency with the facts of spiritual identity. God dependency means that God can be depended on to restore the self which has been buried by exposure to addiction and denial. God dependency illustrates the idea that codependency can be a blessing in disguise. Recognizing that there is a specific name for a set of otherwise vague and uncomfortable feelings can be helpful in the process of healing the disease. Recognizing that daily life should not be controlled by past addictions; recognizing in the midst of confusion, suffering, or feelings of alienation that you need God can be a relief, which some call a blessing.

The practice of God dependency is not confined to participation in a group. It requires no consensus.

God dependency is not "group think."

God dependency is not social behavior or psychological behavior.

God dependency is not another form of codependency.

God dependency is, rather, relying on your own understanding of what a loving God is and does for you. It is a commitment to learn who you are as the child of Spirit, God. This is the discovery of your sacred identity and it is holy work.

Understanding God is the work of ages. But since God wants to be understood, in fact, demands to be understood, just a little bit of understanding, a small amount of faith, a desperate plea for help can bring God into your life. That's what history tells us, what inspiration tells us, what the lives of men and women throughout time tell us.

It's what our own experience tells us. For example, at one time or another, we've all asked ourselves "What do I have to do to get out of this hell?"

It may be a hell as painful as one that includes physical abuse, it may be the hell of chemical abuse, addiction to alcohol or drugs. It may be a crippling and destructive relationship. It may be a hell no more frustrating than a traffic jam on the freeway which keeps you from getting to school or work or home on time. You are a codependent in this situation and you wake up to the anger or danger or frustration or injustice of it all and you say, "Get me out of here, any way you can. *Help.*"

You have just acknowledged your inability to control the situation. You have just acknowledged a Higher Power. You have asked God for freedom from victimization. You have awakened for a moment from a nightmare, and you have recognized that you are in a situation that is not good for you and that you cannot see the way out.

You have started, or renewed, your path to God dependence. You stop feeling helpless for a moment in the understanding that there is probably something that *you* can do to get out of hell. Getting out of hell may mean walking out the door with no money and no coat. It may mean checking in at a hotel and calling a lawyer. It may mean admitting yourself to a rehabilitation center. It may mean leaving your car on the freeway or taking the next off ramp and finding an alternate route, or it may mean making a phone call at the next roadside phone or using the one in your car. Once the Higher Power has been acknowledged a chain reaction begins which feeds you with ideas, motivates your actions, brings a touch of heaven into your life and reminds you that life is worth living.

God dependency can and often does, begin with desperation. Most people find that they are really willing to trust God only when all other methods have failed. But when all else fails, most people reason that nothing can be worse than the hell they are in and so God dependency often begins the same way that the Twelve Steps of AA begin—through an admission of powerlessness.

I know a woman who was at the end of her rope with her husband's drug problem. She had tried and tried—everything she knew to help, solve, let go, forget, trust—and she thought things were getting better. Then she received a call from a woman that her husband had been seeing. "He's taken an overdose," the woman said. "I called the police. He says he wants to die because he can't break the habit."

The wife says, "I was so worn out (exhausted I think, by the problem) that I told her to put my husband on the phone before letting the police take him to the hospital. When I heard him on the other end of the line I told him that he should come home. I told him that I had just made up the bed in the guest room for him."

"And then," she told me, "I picked up my Bible and opened to Matthew—'lo, I am with you always, even unto the end of the world'—and I said, 'Okay. You do it. You are supposed to be here for everyone. You can take care of anything. You take care of this because I absolutely cannot deal with it. I know I am powerless over a drug overdose. This is the end of my world.' "

The police brought the husband home. He was gray and looked like death. He went to bed. So did the wife.

That was a year ago and the man—an addict for ten years— has not touched drugs since. He has regained his health and job and is a fine husband to his wife. He has apologized to the girlfriend and she has a new career and has begun to study more about spiritual life.

The wife says, "I don't know that I can explain what happened. All I know is that treatment, cajoling, threats didn't work. All I know is that I really did turn it over to God and that I believe the Universal Truth touched our personal lives and cast out the demons of drugs."

This woman says that she acknowledged a Higher Power and that she was dependent on someone, something that helped her.

To some that sounds like turning your life over to a total stranger. How can you trust someone or something that you don't know, haven't seen or heard? You wouldn't go to a doctor that you hadn't checked out, you wouldn't send your children to a school whose curriculum was unknown to you, you wouldn't buy a car that you hadn't test driven. You can't or shouldn't rely on a God with whom you are not familiar.

The central issue of codependency and addiction is trust. Whom do you trust? And why? How much trust and where to draw the line between trusting, submitting and having faith are questions that come to the mind, especially when faith and trust have been broken by somebody or something. Sometimes we can't even trust friends or family. How can we trust God, who seems to be a stranger? God dependency explores the issue—the paradox, some say—of faith and trust and looks for understanding.

Two definitions of faith and trust are:

In the widest sense faith means freely accepting what a person says because of one's confidence in that person. That is to say that faith always entails a relationship between persons which stands or falls with the credibility of the person who is believed. In this way faith differs from knowledge which can be proved and from the arbitrary paradox of "blind faith." . . . rather the disclosure appeals to all the dimensions of man so as to order them all to God and its complete fulfillment is love. At the same time God the revealer communicates himself in such a way that this ordering of man to God lays claim to all man's subsequent life; discloses himself both as a lover and as man's surpassing (supernatural), final goal, containing in itself the perfect fulfillment of all hope. (Karl Rahner, *Dictionary of Theology,* 2d ed. [New York: Crossroad, 1981], p. 167)

Faith is a dependence on the truth of another, a firm belief or trust in a person, thing, doctrine or statement. One is said to keep faith when he performs a promise to another.
1. Historically faith is a belief in the truthfulness and accuracy of the Scriptural narrative and teachings.
2. Saving faith is the acceptance by the intellect, affection and will of God's favor extended to man through Christ. This faith produces a sincere obedience in the life and conversation. The firm foundation of faith is the essential supreme affection of God. (*Cruden's Concordance*)

Paradoxically, the recovery from codependency necessitates that the codependent trust in a Higher Power, God. Reliance on a Higher Power means that at some time or another those defined as codependents who want to continue to recover must learn to understand the God they trust. Since the nature of God is a subject of much debate in the world today, this trust often must come with faith. Getting to know God as your best friend is essential in God dependency. If you think that you need something in your life besides yourself, if you have a desperate need for change and you turn your thinking (repent is the biblical word for re-thinking) over to a Higher Power you will want to begin to become acquainted with that Power.

The next step of God dependency is to examine yourself and see how much of your life is spent thinking about yourself and see how much is spent thinking about this God that you have just turned yourself over to. Getting to know God and yourself is essential if you are even thinking about dependence on eternal Spirit, God. Spirit is a biblical name for God and it's no wonder then that the Bible says, "they that worship him must worship him in spirit and in truth."

One of the ways the Bible defines God is as absolute Truth. Honesty is a derivative attribute of Truth and as you are honest with yourself and the people with whom you come in contact you will find that you are experiencing God, the Higher Power in your speech and action. Honesty is a path to the everpresence of God.

Honesty is shown in many ways. It is certainly honest to admit what you cannot do. Somehow we think that we can "do it all," "have it all," and perhaps some people can. I can't. I know that I have a very, very hard time raising four children, working at a full-time job outside the home and trying to have any relationships outside my children that involve more than a few hours' attention at a time. Honestly, I feel I am short-changing everyone if I take on too much.

It would, for me, be dishonest to say that I could do everything and then ask God to help me do it all unless I had checked to hear what God really wanted me to do—if anything.

Forgiveness is a hallmark of God dependency. Forgiving of the self, of others, has been proven over and over to be part of the discovery of God's relationship to daily life. Practical forgiveness involves making amends to those you have wronged and it means forgiving those who have wronged you. Practical forgiveness means letting go of resentment—not holding onto hurt feelings. But the nature of God is forgiveness and so forgiving in relationship to God is not mystical, nor is it particularly difficult when you get the hang of it.

But dependence on God is more than the acknowledgement of powerlessness, more than learning about the nature of God, more than forgiveness.

God dependency involves revising what you think you are. It means revising an understanding of the nature of your self and replacing the narrative (the internal dialogue) of the codependent self with the testimony of spiritual evidence. God dependency ushers in an appreciation that the spiritual evidence is that God needs you, loves you, cares for you, saves you, feeds you, helps you, visits you when you sleep and sends you messages when you are awake.

In biblical Greek the word "thought" is *dialogismos*. It can mean thoughts and reasoning as well as dispute or argument. It's what goes on in our minds when we are confused. Our minds are always talking in thoughts to ourselves. The thoughts we hear can be thoughts that we learned as children; they can be someone else's thoughts, or the words of a song that repeat themselves to us until they disappear or are replaced by others.

God dependency is an active process that replaces the dialogue of the codependent self with the very words of God. The words of God tell us about health and protection and safety and about our sacred self.

Noah and Abraham lived in different centuries from each

other. The voice of instruction that each of them heard was not confined to a particular century. Noah was God dependent when he listened to and acted upon "Make thee an ark." Abraham heard, "Get thee out of thy country" and then packed up for the journey. The instructive voice that can save human life is present in each century—including this one. God dependency replaces the voice of the codependent self with the words of God found in the Bible. God dependency breaks the crippling bonds of codependency and sets free thought and action.

God can, in fact does, speak through the ages. God may be hard to hear through the noise of "You Are Nobody Until Somebody Loves You."

God dependency replaces the lover in the popular song lyrics with the Lover of us all, God, the Higher Power. In God dependency the "you" in "you were always on my mind" is God; "the sweetest thing in all the world is loving You"— Spirit.

God dependency unveils the possibility of seeing and hearing what the world offers in its spiritual dimension. Returning to God as the source of all Creation, all messages, all love, affection and hope, all music and art brings a joy to the heart and soul. Instead of a depressing sense of loss, a sense of God as All fills the heart with completeness. Instead of wandering in the valley of rejection, a sense of God as Father/Mother brings a sense of fullness and prosperity to the human heart.

God dependency means bringing God into human life for the benefit of yourself and the whole world. God dependency means that you are a free moral agent whose foremost task is to understand and apply spirit to your life.

God dependency means not denying your feelings, but

using them to find what God has in mind for you. It means taking frustration, desperation, and desire to the Infinite and watching those frustrations, desperations, and desires transform themselves into a saving action that blesses not only you, but everyone that you come in contact with.

The biblical story of Martha and Mary is the story—in codependency terms—of a classic codependent and her God dependent sister.

Martha is busy, busy, busy, getting the dinner ready, doing good and letting everyone know about it. She is feeling frustrated that her sister is not helping to do what she perceives women and hostesses should be doing. She asks Jesus to tell her sister to get up and get into the kitchen.

The Interpreter's Dictionary of the Bible says, "His (Jesus) precepts in the Sermon on the Mount and elsewhere dealing with human motives and the deep workings of the mind show by implication that he was acutely aware of the place emotional conflict, resentment, fear, anxiety, hatred and the like had in the genesis of disease" (*The Interpreter's Bible*, ed. George Arthur Buttrick, 5 vols. [Nashville, Tenn.: Parthenon Press, 1962], 2:546–47)

Going directly to the heart of God-reliance, Jesus calls Martha by name and says, "Martha, Martha, thou art careful and troubled about many things: But one thing is needful: and Mary hath chosen that good part, which shall not be taken away from her" (Luke 10:41–42, AV). And the next thing recorded, according to Luke's account, is that Jesus taught people to pray, "Our Father which art in heaven, Hallowed be thy name. Thy kingdom come. Thy will be done as in heaven, so in earth."

Later Jesus said, "The Kingdom of heaven is within you."

Martin Buber says, "Some religions do not regard our sojourn on earth as true life. They either teach that everything appearing to us here is mere appearance, behind which we should penetrate, or that it is only a forecourt of the true world, a forecourt which we should cross without paying much attention to it ' . . . the two worlds are essentially one' " (*The Way of Man* [Secaucus N.J.: Citadel Press, 1966], p. 39).

The world that we live in includes codependency and it includes a desire to understand God. It includes millions and millions of people who have turned to God to help them with addiction, codependency and their daily lives. The turning point for these millions was dependence on God as they understood Him.

The main points of God dependency as described in this book are that:

The Bible is for everyone, regardless of denomination or belief structure.

The Bible is easily understood in the language of life today.

The Bible is relevant to life today.

The Bible offers answers to your problems.

Individuals can read and study the Bible for themselves without fear of offending God or the church.

Reading the Bible as an individual heals the self and its diseases.

Dependence on God is not blind faith in an irrational Being.

Twelve Steps Toward GodDependency

1. I will not continue my codependency by using the same words over and over. God is the Word and is Infinite; therefore as the occasion demands, I can find new words to express God and my relationship to God and to my problems and the problems of the world.

2. If I feel that I am hearing the same stories over and over I will look and diligently search for an antidote to repetitiveness.

3. I will tell the truth.

4. I will love my neighbor as myself. I will not recoil in fear nor congratulate myself that someone else's story is worse than mine.

5. I will not project my fears or the fears of society on my neighbors at home, in church and in the world. I will cast the beam out of my own eye first.

6. God speaks to me.

7. I listen.

8. I understand.

9. Trust is what I must learn.

10. Faith is what I practice.

11. I don't react to my own fears. I think and feel God.

12. I deserve Love.

5

The Nature of God as Love, Spirit, Truth, Peace

I'm a hard case. I didn't understand the nature of God at all until I actually saw the healing through prayer of physical symptoms. One day they were all there—diagnosed by a doctor. The next day they were gone.

What I learned from that experience was that the only thing I knew was that I didn't know anything.

All my education, all my reading, all my conversations hadn't told me what I learned through that healing. Study hadn't told me that God was All. That God would be, not something out there or up there, but *in my very life.*

I realized that it was a life's work to understand God. I knew that it would take forever to figure out God in my life. I don't know whether anyone understands God more than in part before the day called forever, but I certainly knew then and know now that it is going to take me forever.

Jesus, whose understanding of God caused people to call him Messiah, whose works caused people to start churches named after him, who has been called the Son of God by people through the ages said that his doctrine was not really his but that of "Him who sent me."

That "Him" that Jesus refers to I interpret to be the I Am who spoke to Moses on the mountain out of the burning bush. I interpret that Him to be the same presence as the one who is described as saying, "As a mother comforteth her children so will I comfort you."

I interpret God through the Bible.

This is hardly revolutionary, although it seems so to some. I believe that the Bible is the Word of God, that it is a record of the history of men and women and their relationship to God, that it contains the answer to the most profound question of the ages: "Who am I?"

That's the question Jesus asked Peter, and on the third try Peter got it right when he said, "Thou art the Christ, the Son of the living God" (Mt. 16:16, AV). How one interprets who one is and what church is depends on inspiration, revelation and study of at least the Greek and Hebrew words for Christ, son, life and God in every reference in which they appear in the Bible. Anyone interested in the answer to these questions should look in the Bible Concordance and into the life and attitudes of Peter as related in the Bible before any comment is made or accepted on what Peter's answer means.

I haven't done that. I don't really know what Peter's answer means, although I have some of my own ideas on it. What I do know is that "Who am I?" is the question that Jesus asked for all of us.

"Who am I?" is something that we all want to know.

How we find that out is a process. It's like checkers.

You can't make two moves at once, you may only move forward and not backward until you get to the other side, from where you can move wherever you like.

The nature of God as I understand God at the moment is described in the Bible. God is Love. God is Truth. God is Spirit. God is at hand. God is Good.

I know that God moves upon the face of the waters and I believe that God parts the Red Sea—the obstacles to our progress.

Betty K. believes that she learned about the nature of God not through the words of the Bible but through forgiveness.

Betty still cries—years after the night that is hard for her to talk about. Her husband worked all week. He was successful. He was home. He didn't beat his wife or children, but he drank and drank on the weekends until the whole fabric of Betty's life was torn.

As a Christian, Betty kept forgiving him. She thought if she let it go he would get better, stop drinking.

Her husband started blaming her for things that she knew weren't her fault. He threatened her. He had told her before that if she went to a Twelve Step support group he would leave her, but now she was at her wit's end.

She did go. She snuck out of the house and met with two other women—women she would never otherwise meet, women from a different social class and with a different skin color who told her that she should go ahead and cry and tell them whatever she wanted. "We've heard it all," one of the women said. Betty poured her heart out and admitted that she was afraid and didn't know what to do.

She tells now how that night she was lying cautiously in bed next to her husband and how she felt her body tighten up, "Shrink, kinda," she says now with her southern drawl. "I just felt that I had to get very close together, my arms next to my hips, and that I had to hold on and the next thing I knew I felt my spirit leave my body and go into my husband's."

As she wipes the tears from hers eyes with a luncheon napkin, Betty says, "I know it's hard to believe and I'm not sure that these are really the words to explain what happened, but I felt his pain. God, it was terrible. I'd never felt anything like it before. It was just for a few seconds, moments, I don't know how long, not long really, but I felt this horrible anguish and I couldn't believe a person could hurt so much. Then I was back in my own body."

"Well, what happened," she says, "is the next day at noon he said he was going to quit drinking and he would go to an AA meeting and he did. And the thing is, I have never, never held a grudge against him from that moment to this. I forgave him everything that instant that I felt his pain. And my poise was restored and I was able to deal with whatever came up, and things did, although heaven knows I've not had the problems that some people have. But I could forgive him for everything that he had done because I knew just how much he hurt."

Betty's experience is beyond empathy. Her flesh became one with her husband's in some very mystical sense and that union healed both of them and sent her and her husband to the Twelve Steps and sobriety.

Sobriety is a state of mind say Twelve Step members. The key to the State of Sobriety is the desire to turn one's rights as a citizen over to a Higher Power. The acknowledgment of the absolute sovereignty of Divine Mind, Love, Truth, Spirit is the first step into the realm of sobriety.

Usually the only people willing to relinquish those sovereign rights are people who have lost control of themselves and are forced to lean on something other than the ego. The sick are the first to turn to God.

To live in a state of mind in which you are not the center of the universe is a step toward sobriety. To enter into a state of sobriety is to pass through the gates to heaven, where God is sovereign.

Twelve Step members are trying to break the hellish patterns instilled in them by their families and to be reborn as functioning, clear-thinking, independent adults.

Sally told me that she was in a meeting of JACS, Jewish Alcoholics and Codependents, and that she realized, as the group gathered to hold hands and repeat the twenty-third Psalm, that it was a prohibition for the Hasidic rabbi beside her to take her hand, as by tradition he is allowed to touch women only when they are members of his immediate family.

Being a twentieth-century woman with the wisdom of Esther in her bones, Sally did not offer to move but asked the rabbi if he would be more comfortable somewhere else in the circle.

"The rabbi turned to me," says Sally, "and he hugged me."

"Here," he said, "my sobriety is my number one concern. Out there," he motioned with his hand, "there is another set of rules. In here it's something else." And he hugged Sally again and held her hand while they repeated,

The Lord is my shepherd;
I lack nothing,
He makes me lie down in green pastures;
He leads me to water in places of repose;
He renews my life;
He guides me in right paths as befits His name.
Though I walk through a valley of deepest darkness,
I fear no harm, for You are with me;
Your rod and Your staff—they comfort me.
You spread a table for me in full view of my enemies;
You anoint my head with oil;
My drink is abundant;
Only goodness and steadfast love shall pursue me
all the days of my life,
and I shall dwell in the house of the LORD
for many long years.

(Psalm 23, *Tanakh—The Holy Scriptures* [New York: Jewish Publication Society, 1985]used by permission of the Jewish Publication Society)

A longing for sobriety had caused the rabbi to drop his formal patterns in favor of new behavior and responses—and new ways of looking at things.

"So now, do not be afraid; I myself will provide for you and your dependents" (Genesis 50:21, *The Bible: An AmericanTranslation* [Chicago: University of Chicago Press, 1949]).

That's what Joseph said to his brothers, and his story and his words are where forgiveness first appears by name in the Bible.

Joseph's brothers threw him into a pit, then sold him into slavery. Many years later, after they were near starvation, he had fed them and forgiven them and moved them to Egypt under his protection, but only after their father Jacob died did they ask Joseph's forgiveness. Their motivation was suspect and less than honorable but undeniably self-preserving.

Realizing that their father was dead, Joseph's brothers said, "Suppose Joseph should take an aversion to us, and pay us back for all the harm that we did him!"

So they sent a message to Joseph, saying, "Before his death your father gave this command: 'Thus shall you say to Joseph: "Pray forgive the crime and sin of your brothers in doing you harm."' So now, please forgive the crime of the servants of your father's God."

Joseph wept . . . (and) said to them,

"Do not be afraid; for can I take God's place? You meant to do me harm, but God has accounted it good, in order to do as he has done today: save the lives of many people." (Genesis 50:15–20, AT)

God saves lives today. It's the nature of God to save life and to give it more abundantly and if we want to understand the nature of God we must search the Scriptures for ourselves and find what is there for us.

If we want to understand how to deal with addiction, codependency, with all our relationships, with our national problems, with our churches we must understand the nature of God for ourselves or we will remain codependent and keep on repeating fruitless behavior patterns.

We must discover God for ourselves if we want to discover spiritual self-reliance. We can discover God in a group, or we can discover God in the silence of Spirit wherever we are. But to discover the nature of God and our spiritual, sacred self we must silence the dialogue of our senses, we must stop arguing with ourselves on both sides of the fence, we must give up our belief that we are isolated in shame and that we are damaged from youth and always missing the mark because we descended from Adam and Eve.

We are released from the bondage of Adam and Eve, and from the suffering that follows their mythological actions as surely as Joseph and his brothers lived in the Egypt that is beyond Jordan in the Nile River Valley thousands of years ago, as surely as their descendents were led by Moses through the Red Sea.

We must practice what we know.

We know we want God in our lives, we know we want freedom from our own personal hell.

God dependency, understanding the nature of God, takes practice.

"Model your conduct on what you have learned from me, on what I have told you and shown you, and you will find that the God of peace will be with you" (Philippians 4:9, *The New Testament in Modern English*, J.B. Phillips, translator).

Peace, says the Bible, is God's nature.

6

God, AA, and Religion:
Where We Go Next

It is a well known fact that in terms of numbers and societal effect, the most remarkable and successful treatment of alcohol and drug addiction of our times is found in the Twelve Steps of Alcoholics Anonymous.

In a world where attention is focused on addiction and the tangled relationships in families and between men and women, AA meetings are a beacon of hope. In the basements of churches, in YM-and YWCA buildings, in community centers throughout the nation, AA-related meetings have become a gathering place where the sick, weary and suffering are turning for companionship, inspiration, support, healing, comfort. In the minds of many, the AA program, with its emphasis on God and healing of addiction, has become part of the religious revival of this last half-century.

Many people in AA feel that a prayer to God led them not to church but to AA. They found that AA helped them when nothing else did. They find in the Twelve Step program a way to maintain an identity free from substance abuse and a way to put God into their daily life.

Since its first meetings fifty years ago, millions of people in Alcoholics Anonymous have found that the way out of the specific hell of alcohol addiction is a process characterized by the following approach:

1. acknowledge powerlessness over alcohol
2. admit to something more powerful than yourself
3. turn life over to God as you understand Him
4. examine yourself
5. be honest with yourself and at least one other person
6. be willing to have God remove your shortcomings
7. be humble
8. seek forgiveness
9. make amends
10. pray continually to do only the will of God
11. put into practice what you learn
12. spread the word

This process of acknowledgement, turning life over to the Higher Power, this process of self-examination, willingness to trust God, humility, forgiveness, prayer, practice and the sharing of the good news of healing is the attitude of the Bible toward prayer. The process of the Twelve Steps is the process illustrated in the Lord's Prayer as given by Jesus Christ in the gospel of Matthew.

Of the Twelve Steps, five speak of God directly. Five call for actions based on an acknowledgement and understanding of God and of people's relationship to each other. The first step of the program is an admission—in the words of Jesus—that "I can of mine own self do nothing" (John 5:30, AV).

Working with the attitudes and actions of these steps, millions of people who previously suffered from active alcoholism are recovering from its ravages and discovering a new relationship to God. Participating in the process of acknowledgement, honesty, forgiveness and communication, drunks have become sober.

The Twelve Step programs of Alcoholics Anonymous have changed the way millions of people think about themselves. Alcoholics and their families have, to a great degree, stopped thinking about alcoholism as a sin and about themselves as sinners wandering from place to place with the burden of addiction. This thinking has been replaced by the concept of addiction as disease and God as a benevolent Higher Power.

The concept of a judgmental deity gives way in AA programs to the concept of a Higher Power that can be defined in any way one best understands at the moment. Many AA members feel that the AA group they are in at the moment is the Higher Power.

God is being redefined each day by millions of individuals in thousands of Twelve Step meetings. As a result of this continual populist redefinition of God, the Twelve Steps of AA may have as profound an effect on the popular theology of our times as the 95 Theses of Martin Luther did on his.

A changed perception as to the nature of God and sin has changed the way people think about the role of religion in their lives. No denominational God intrudes itself into AA meetings. There is no minister or priest or authority figure there to interpret God on Sundays or religious holidays. There are no building programs or fund-raising drives, and the only money collected (and not every group collects money) is for the few basic expenses of each particular meeting.

Families of alcoholics were the first contemporary group of people to recognize that addiction is "crazy-making" for everyone involved. They recognized that no man, woman or child is an island, but that what affects one of us affects another. They identified the multi-generational impact of alcohol addiction with its effects, even to the third and fourth generation.

In order to recover from addiction codependents admit

that they are powerless over not just alcohol but the alcoholic as well. Through the literature and conversation of codependency and addiction, they learn that they have been acting out roles in a drama scripted, directed, and produced by alcohol. Codependents in AA-related meetings discover that they are not players in the unfolding story of their own unique life but players, rather, in a soap opera of addiction. In AA-related meetings they learn that in order to recover from addiction they must admit the reality of their addiction, turn their lives over to God and work for understanding and freedom from the evils of alcohol and addiction.

Finding freedom from the devastating effects of alcoholism was what Dr. Bob Smith and Bill Wilson had in mind in 1935 when they founded Alcoholics Anonymous. Both men were alcoholics. They spoke each other's language—they had had the same experiences, fears and failures. They had tried prayer, they had tried church, they had tried pastoral counselling, medicine, hospitals, and will power. And they were still drunks. What they had not tried was absolute reliance on an all-powerful God. Suffering and experience brought them to the realization that nothing but God has power to control the lives of addicted human beings. They turned their lives over to a Higher Power.

This was no media event. No television cameras were there to catch their words. This was a private moment between two men who needed more help than the world had offered, men who found peace and hope in a quiet moment in the home of a woman who loved God. What survives of that exchange between the two men is the testimony of the participants, written down and passed around at first by word of mouth; and a movement that has touched the lives of millions and continues, to this day, to grow.

By 1939 Bill Wilson and Dr. Bob were both sober, had saved hundreds of others and had developed a guidebook. The guidebook listed the Twelve Steps for recovery from alcohol and recounted testimonies from people healed of their addiction to liquor and of its effects on the home and children in the home.

The guidebook—those testimonies, compiled with the Twelve Steps that the men developed - is commonly known as "The Big Book." Its formal name is *Alcoholics Anonymous*—the name a magazine writer gave to the movement. The book is subtitled, *The Story of How Many Thousands of Men and Women Have Recovered from Alcoholism.* Its 347 pages recount many stories of alcoholism, healings of alcoholism, acknowledgements of the Higher Power, God, Love, Mind, and sincere expressions of gratitude for the freedom found in conjunction with that power.

If it sounds as if AA has something to do with religion, it does. Its two founders were Christians, members of a group endeavoring to practice primitive Christianity. It is not beyond the imagination to consider that these men, who knew and had studied the gospel texts, heard the words of the New Testament resonating in their consciousness as they talked of God and reexamined together their beliefs about Him.

In a departure from the approach of organized religion, there were no propositional statements about the nature of God. It was a simple matter to start with "God as we understood Him." It was simple to start with whatever understanding of God anyone had at the moment of surrender to God.

As they drew up the Twelve Steps of AA they consulted with ministers and those familiar with the Bible. It comes as no surprise that the Twelve Steps are based on the spirit of the instructions of Jesus Christ: "This, therefore, is the way you are to pray."

The Twelve Steps are adaptations to alcohol abuse of the spirit of those statements of Jesus referred to by much of the church as the Lord's Prayer.

There is, in both statements, an acknowledgement of God, the Higher Power, our universal father, as able to control what we are unable to control—the heavens and the earth, as well as alcohol.

There is, in both statements, the necessity for forgiveness of ourselves and others. There is, in both, the affirmation of the need for deliverance from evil, the Evil One.

The Twelfth Step reads very much as a spreading of the Gospel of spiritual awakening and an injunction to put in practice what has been learned—in every event of daily life. And because millions have followed the Twelve Steps and have spread the word, now, some fifty years after the development of the fellowship of Alcoholics Anonymous, the Twelve Step programs have taken hold in the consciousness of much of the nation. Millions have discovered that the Twelve Steps heal not only addiction to alcohol, but to drugs, and to unhealthy family and political and church relationships.

In the half century since the first meeting of Bill Wilson and Dr. Bob the power involved in what the two men forged in the library of a middle western home during the Depression years has spread to the point where—if the success of a community is counted in numbers—AA programs have a record of growth that many church denominations would envy.

Some say that is the companionship AA meetings offer that makes the program effective. Others say that it is the ability to define the problem, enforce honesty, focus on realistic goals, the support of a community of friends and peers with special understanding and empathy. Others say it is the power of the Lord's Prayer and God at work today.

But whatever the rationale, the fact is that by adhering to and working with the Twelve Steps of Alcoholics Anonymous millions and millions of men, women and children have found freedom. The crippling effects of addiction to chemical substances and to a life with those involved in substance abuse are removed or mitigated by a power greater than chemical substance, family patterns, medicine, political or denominational loyalties.

"I'm Scott, and I am a recovering alcoholic," the man on my left at a Virginia dinner party said to me. "What do you do?" I told him that I was writing a book on codependency and he said, pointing to the woman on my right, "That's my codep over there."

As I introduced myself to the woman, she said that her name was Daphne and that she and her husband had just returned from a month at the Hazelden Family Institute program.

Scott had been raised in an alcoholic home. An affable, open, and friendly man, Scott invited me to a meeting of a local ACoA (Adult Children of Alcoholics) group and told me that he was a practicing Christian.

Daphne and Scott were Episcopalians and they were worried about their priest. "He's a great organizer," Daphne said, "but he's a terrible people person. He has absolutely no ability to get along with people. I think that the congregation is the enabler here."

In AA language Daphne meant that by keeping the priest on at the church she, her husband, and the congregation were allowing the priest to continue in what appeared to her unfriendly ways. Faithful churchgoer though she was, she used the language, not of the Eucharist nor of the Common Prayer, but of AA. Living with an alcoholic and attending Twelve Step meetings had given her an AA perspective that carried over to church.

AA had given her words to describe her priest, and a concept that had changed her perspective. She saw a codependent congregation which was under the influence of the priest. She felt, not that the congregation needed more spirituality or a deeper recognition of its pastor, but that the priest should go.

I went to an ACoA meeting with Scott some time after my conversation with him and Daphne, and this is what I heard. "I couldn't go to church without feeling angry," the woman in the red shirt said. It was a Sunday night and she was one of twenty women and men in one of the countless thousands of ACoA groups meeting daily throughout the nation. "I would sit there and look around me and see the hypocrisy and I'd be so mad that I wanted to get up and walk out. The preaching was about one thing and the lives lived by my fellow church members were about another," she said, looking at each member of the group for support.

"And then I found these Twelve Step meetings where it's possible to talk openly, to say what is on my mind with no fear of judgement. I found that I was not alone, and the strangest thing has happened. As I came to these meetings, as I got in touch with my self-esteem, I have been able to go back to church and now I really am happy there. And when I'm not," she added, "I let them know how I really feel. It's amazing."

"Just this morning," she continued, her smiling face warming the room, "I was supposed to teach a class on 'Keeping the Inner Vessel Clean' and I told the group that I didn't like the title, that I thought it was irrelevant language and I told them about the struggle of the self that I am treating, that is being treated here in these meetings. I can't tell you how many people came up to me afterward and told me that they really appreciated my honesty."

"Honesty is what these meetings are about," responded a woman on the other side of the circle. "Honesty is spiritual power," said another "and that's what these meetings of Adult Children of Alcoholics are about—finding spiritual power."

"I think what has happened," said the woman in the red shirt, "is that what I've gotten at these meetings is something that I take back to my church. It's changed things for me there."

"AA-related meetings are primitive Christianity," says Ted L. with conviction. Ted attends three to six meetings a week as well as Sunday church services where he has served for twenty years in every lay capacity his church offers. And although he has been a faithful churchgoer for two decades, it was not church, not the liturgy, not his priest who stopped his drinking or who helped him bind up his broken heart. "I was born again on June 9, 1983 at 12:15," he says. "That's the minute, the day, that I decided to go to AA." It was AA and ACoA and Al-Anon and a month in family therapy at Hazelden Institute in Minnesota that put him not only on the path to his own wellness, but to a new understanding and appreciation of Christianity.

"These meetings," he says, with the authority of the lawyer and leader in his community that he is, "are to me what it must have been like for the early Christians. Meeting whenever and wherever we can to share the good news about healing, about a Higher Power which can help, a God, a Love, that feels for me and helps me control and understand my life."

"Well, I still have real problems with the idea of a

Christian God up there, a Him who is helping me," said another man. "God never helped me when I asked Him as a child to stop my mother's drinking. I think of God as the Universe with its own sense of good, and control in cycles, more or less. I suppose," he added as an afterthought, "it's sort of a Buddhist concept as well as an astro-physicist's concept."

Another woman in the circle of fellowship on this Sunday evening in a medium-size southern city said, "I'm interested that we all talk about God as a Him. The Bible talks about God as Mother in the Psalms and in Isaiah, and I wish that we could explore that idea more."

"I can't stand the idea of God," said a tall, handsome, troubled man to her left. "He never helped me, and I don't understand all those relentless readings and printed prayers."

A woman to his left, comfortably seated on a sofa with two of her friends said, "I don't think you can blame God. After all, He has brought you this far. I have an entirely different point of view. When my father left," she said, "the priest came to our house two nights a week for years and he played poker with us or sat around and talked, and he saved my mother and my sisters and me. I thought of him as a Christ-figure and I still do. I couldn't marry unless he was there. It was important to me that the Christ-figure was present at my wedding."

She turned again to the troubled man sprawled across his chair. "Was there ever a time that you liked church?" she asked. "Well," he said, reflecting, "when I was in college I used to go into the chapel and just sit there in the silence and I really liked that. The candles were lit and there was a serenity and a peace that I did find there." His face contorted as he added, "But I can't stand being preached at about all that sin and stuff. I don't like being manipulated."

"I apply the AA motto to that kind of talk," said a young career woman in the group. "I take what I want and leave the rest. I won't listen to false theology any more. God is Love and that's that."

One woman commented that the Bible identifies God as Love, and then members of the group started giving Biblical definitions of God: Truth, Light, Love, Spirit, Eternal, Only, Holy, Not a Man, Refuge, Judge, Helper, With Us, Life, Mother, Father, the Word, Presence, Power.

Twenty people sitting in a circle talking about a Higher Power had begun to discover that each of the myriad number of ways God is described opens doors of the mind.

Take my word for it, sitting in a room where the doors and windows of minds closed by fear, by shame, by passions, false education, and false doctrine are opening to the Light that Exists is a religious experience of the first order.

By their presence at the meeting these people were saying that codependency must be denied the right to control lives. They were saying that individuality must be resurrected if the self is to become what it is called to be.

They were exploring the possibilities of using their feelings to lead them to a Higher Power. They were challenging church and taking to it what they had learned in AA meetings. These people were discovering that life is not meant to be a nightmare of codependency, but rather that codependency can bring one to being and power that awakens in an individual struggling to express spiritual sense, to find a life of peace.

Recovering addicts and codependents can relate to Martin Buber's description of Hasidism, a particular spiritual approach to God and life: "A man should himself realize that conflict-situations between himself and others are nothing but the effects of conflict-situations in his own soul; then he should try to overcome this inner conflict, so that afterwards he may go out to his fellow-men and enter into new, transformed relations with them." (*The Way of Man* [Secaucus, N.J.: Citadel Press, 1966], p. 28)

We are a nation of individuals and a nation of congregations and political and moral persuasions. We divide ourselves into believers and non-believers, denominations and sects and cults. Ninety-four percent of us claim to believe in some kind of Higher Power, God. Over sixty percent of us don't know where on the world map to find the United States.

But if half of us don't know where we live on the world map how can we know where the Higher Power dwells?

We are a nation that claims to be under God but a nation of few who, when asked, can define God. Those who do claim to know are called everything from ideologues to great leaders.

How God is defined and by whom makes a difference in the political and the religious world. If God is the ultimate power, then who else has a right to power? Those who do God's will? Who defines God's will? You? Or someone else?

Codependents are letting someone else define—or be— God for them. Spiritually self-reliant persons define God in the language of Spirit. They pray, study, reflect and practice actively a growing understanding of Spirit, Love, Truth. They recognize the symptoms of addiction and codependency as the death of the self, the potential rebirth of the spiritual self and the spiritual sense of church.

"Groups modeled on Alcoholics Anonymous have a strong spiritual orientation: at meetings members acknowledge the existence of a higher power and accept their own powerlessness over their addictions. Many attend meetings every week and believe they will continue to do so throughout their lives, much as they might go to church or temple," says Trish Hall in the *New York Times* (October 7, 1988, Section B, p. 8).

"We are first century Christians," says Bill H., who told me that he felt that Twelve Step programs were like meetings of early Christians, in that people in the Twelve Step programs are like-minded people, people who have been healed or stopped drinking or curbed or eradicated their addictions by basing their life on a Higher Power, on an all-good, all-powerful God. What it means to him is that there are no priests to interpret for them, their hearts are alive with worship, they have a deep sense of community in ministering to each other and to themselves. What they know is that they have seen a possibility of new life, that they have in some sense been resurrected.

Some of these people attend or belong to a denominational church, others do not. But to a person, what they get in the meetings is something that they say they do not get in church. What they get is a sense of understanding of their emotions and life problems that is based on experience. What they get is community, based on common symptoms and problems and not on doctrine.

The focus of an AA meeting is not the interpretation of the interpretation of a man from another time; as, for example, a discussion of the role of service as seen by John Wesley, or the question of faith as detailed by Martin Luther. The focus of an AA meeting is not the future condition of a man's soul, but rather how to get through the next hour without taking a drink.

The time in AA meetings is not spent thinking about the building fund, about the bishop's wife, about the failure of some members of the congregation to live up to the high standards of the church. It is spent, rather, talking about how people lie to themselves, about how mad they are or how grateful they are to be alive.

The immediate focus is the dialogue of the mind (the lies people tell themselves) that leads to addiction. The meeting is about how to recognize the symptoms, the suggestions, the serious craziness of addiction.

It is impossible to let the mind wander in a Twelve Step meeting. The stories of the alcoholics or of the children of alcoholics are wrenching. To hear them, seeing men and women talk of their experiences as a result of alcohol or other intoxicants, is to hear every pain the world has offered, every degradation that flesh and blood can suffer. The stories of alcoholics make television mini-series or soap operas look like a quick glimpse of nursery school.

People in the meetings speak the truth in plain language, the language of the day. Anyone who has ever attended a meeting has heard there all manner of expression from the language of the street to the language of the locker room, board room, kitchen and bedroom.

What they get is in plain language. What they get is a sense of equality with each other through sharing their pain. What they get is some release of guilt and shame by sharing their grief and anger in front of others. What they get is hope for improvement in this lifetime.

What they don't get is preaching. What they don't get is a sense that women are less important than men. What they don't get is that one political party is better than another. What they don't get are appeals for promotion money. What they don't get is a sense of hierarchy.

What they also don't get are some wonderful things; the

rich imagery of the church, the stories and examples of the prophets and the penitents, the heroes and heroines of the Bible. What they don't get is education on the movement of men and nations in the light of history, in the light of the Eternal. What they don't get is tradition—the familiar which binds us together in celebration and communion and elevates the heart. What they don't get is the good news that healing can come overnight, in the twinkling of an eye. What they generally don't get is the wisdom of the ages in the language of its most beautiful poets, daring politicians, far-sighted prophets—the language of its oracles. Some wonderful things await them.

The meeting can go no higher than the highest thought being expressed at any one time. And if someone in the group has had a breakthrough, taken a step out of the morass of codependency, made a leap of faith, then everyone at the meeting benefits. If the Higher Power of the group speaks to them all it is a Pentecost experience, not unlike that recorded in the Book of Acts where each person heard the message of the Holy Spirit in his or her own language—as it applied individually.

In a culture conditioned to fifteen-second sound bites, to quick images appealing to the psychology of the individual as a market research object dependent on the senses and passions to function, people do not hear discourses by William Jennings Bryan, words of inspiration from Walt Whitman, reflections on Creation by Paul.

Rather, the language of the Twelve Step programs is in the national air. "Enabling, caretaking, lost child and code-pendency" have become words to describe human behavior.

I've never been to a church meeting where people talked about inviting a man over to spend the night in bed, where someone said they hated their mother.

There may be such churches but I have never been to one. People who attend church generally do not attend to expose the details of their life. They attend for countless reasons, but self-exposure in public is not one of them as far as I know. Church, for many, is a sanctuary from the ills of the age, as are AA Twelve Step meetings.

There is a point at which the great river of religious men, women and children of this country joins the great river of people in the Twelve Step community. It is at this juncture that we, as a community of seekers, a nation of churches, now stand. This juncture is the place described in the Book of Acts where each person understood the other in their own language. It is the place where Moses stood when he heard the voice of God out of the burning bush. Collectively, as a nation, the place where we stand is holy ground. The trick is to recognize it.

Experts in the area of codependency have done Christians a service when they have pointed out the possibilities of codependent behavior in churches and families. By identifying such behavior they have made it possible to think about recovering the original Spirit of the message of the Bible.

The insights, testimonies, the gratitude, the faith, trust, and hope, and humility that are embodied in the words of the congregation of believers in Twelve Step programs are a call to action to the churches and to individuals in the churches.

The need for healing has galvanized the nation, there is a spiritual seeker on every corner, in every home, apartment and temporary shelter on this planet. We see them in front of us every day.

Where to find the answer to pain, to hurt, to problems is the question.

Some people, even people in churches, feel that the Spirit of the church is often clothed in the dead letter of cant and hollow ritual. Those who have found churches that stimulate their thought, increase their ability to heal, serve their brother and sister and neighbor; churches that strengthen the position of women and children and the helpless of society are rare.

Those who have found churches that reflect the beauty and originality and harmony and order of Soul, that nourish the individual sense of walking with the ever-present love of the Holy Spirit are rarer still.

This is the kind of church that most people want, long for, search for. It is a non-addictive church.

It does not count on the personality of any one individual to rouse it, or inform it, or govern it, or guide it, or control it.

It does not require large buildings designed to impress. It does not keep itself busy in the activities of the world with bowling alleys and movie theaters and dances and endless socializing. Its motivation is the Spirit of Truth and Love and its members are occupied with spiritual study and reflection and subsequent action and practical concern for the fatherless and widows.

In this admittedly ideal church there is little or no dissension among its members. They respect each others' opinions, listen to each other with deep and abiding interest, care for each other as the very burning flame of the living Truth through the ages.

It is a church based on washing each other's feet, understanding how far each and every one of our fellow citizens has come on their own unique and individual path toward spiritual sense. It is not trying to impress the world with its proficiency and rightness.

It is not a church that fosters codependent behavior.

One of the Judeo-Christian concepts used to cripple women's ability to think and act and move properly is that she is born a sinner because Eve ate a piece of fruit that someone, not God, told her they weren't supposed to eat. That concept is not found in the first story of Creation in Genesis 1:1-2:4 and anyone in this day and age who still believes that women are divinely ordained to be subject to men has not looked deeply enough into the Bible.

It is quite clear that in this telling and believing many Christian women become codependents. They become addicted because they want to believe in Truth and are told, and trust, untruths. Women might as well believe the earth is flat as believe that the Bible supports male domination.

Even without the concept of Eve, women are still subjugated—in the Far East, the Middle East, on the sub-continent. Women know that they are judged by society to be inferior. They make less money. They have to work harder. They hear that girl children in China are drowned at birth. They read the surveys that say most people would rather have a boy child than a girl child. They experience incest, rape; or they know about it from their friends. They see men making decisions that affect global peace and their lives and the lives of their children. Women know.

Women feel limited and their spirituality is suppressed when they are not treated equally, or when they are patronized as "the little woman."

Although few things are more pleasant to any woman than to make a man happy, religious women have been held captive by an illusion. The Bible does not claim superiority of male over female. The Bible describes incidences of male force victimizing women. It also describes females wielding power and subduing men and nations, and defines God as Mother.

Women in a codependent relationship to church, to men, are shortchanging themselves, their churches, their nation, and the Truth that they love. And at some level of their being they know it.

Yet there is no particular freedom to be found in saying that it is the fault of men that things are the way they are in the world any more than it is to assume that women are the cause of all the mess. At this point in history it is not a question of whose fault it is, but what to do about the fear and the codependent and addictive behavior that results from fear.

Many women are still reluctant to challenge a man, most particularly in the field of religion where canonized interpretation has traditionally belonged to men. These women are often called feminists as if it were a dirty word.

It is worth repeating that recognizing the symptoms of codependency is important in the same way that it is important to recognize any disease or destructive pattern of behavior. Fruitless patterns repeat themselves. If the fruitless pattern of codependency is not recognized it continues unchecked and untreated and unhealed. Codependency recognized can be dealt with and can lead the psyche to demand a more practical cogent explanation of the role of God in daily life. It can lead to churches which address the issues raised by codependency.

In the search for a church adequate to today's needs and today's culture there exists an oasis for many millions in the Twelve Step programs.

But for the people that I have talked to in these programs and in the programs that I have attended there seems to be confusion about exactly where to find the next watering spot on life's journey. They say, and one hears at all meetings, that they are not sure what the next step in spiritual growth really is. Who is listening to this inquiry?

In the churches the self that is wounded, denied, frustrated—trying to find relief—turns toward the texts of the Judeo-Christian culture and the leadings and interpretations of church officials.

In the Twelve Step programs, breaking the bad habits of codependent reaction depends on defining God for yourself, for the self that needs help.

It is at this point that if church members are open to their own message they have an opportunity to reach out, to redefine the approach of the church and to come together with the sincere people in the Twelve Step programs, just as the Twelve Steppers have included church members seeking healing.

The churches can come together with the Twelve Step community to define God anew for this age. They can do more than let AA meetings use the basement or community meeting rooms. They can listen and learn and share the similarities and particulars of understanding God.

Acknowledgement of a Higher Power is something both groups claim to do. Acknowledgement of forgiveness, honesty and trust in Spirit are the hallmarks of the age. They are the sign of all peoples seeking God, Love.

A best-selling novel published a few years ago popularized the notion that love means never having to say you're sorry.

Wrong.

Love always means having to say that you are sorry. Without an admission of our wrongs there is no possibility of real, vibrant, fulfilling, and transforming love. Sorry. We all wish it were otherwise. But forgiveness does transform and forgiveness is more than saying you are sorry.

Forgiveness is also much, much more than letting others

off the hook.

Forgiveness involves, among other things, some perception of the total power of Good to clear away everything from
minor misunderstandings to the horrors that one people can
perpetrate on another.

It does this not by excusing wrongs. Forgiveness is not
a salve to put over open wounds. Forgiveness looks in another
direction entirely, a direction unknown to the banality of evil.
It looks toward a Higher Power and puts one's trust and faith
there.

The forgiveness of Jesus, shown and spoken (Father
forgive them, they know not what they do) as he was sweating
drops of blood while nailed to a cross was not a passive,
wimpy forgiveness. René Girard, in his book *The Scapegoat*,
discusses Jesus on the cross and the recognition there of the
collective unconscious at work. Girard says that as a people
we haven't yet caught up with the Resurrection—or even
Creation.

The record of human history evidences that where there
is no forgiveness there is no peace and no prosperity, no
security and no hope.

Hope and forgiveness—expectancy of good, under
whatever name, is a foundation stone of spiritual self-reliance.

Forgiveness is central to Christianity and to the Twelve
Step programs. Forgiveness is the path to healing codependency and addiction wherever they are found.

The challenges of codependency and addiction are as
real and as present as the slavery of the Israelites in Egypt
hundreds of years after Joseph had left the scene. The path out
of the national and individual slavery of codependency and
addiction may be as long and as arduous as when Moses and
Aaron and Miriam led the people through the wilderness, but

the covenant of God with the people today is no less sure. The manna in the wilderness is still with us.

That manna can be seen as the Word speaking to us today in our particular needs, in the midst of our particular emotions. The I Am that revealed itself to Moses unites the mercy and justice of the Higher Power with the affections of the heart and mind to bring about a better life, a more peaceful land, quiet and calm in the storm of the past, the present, and the future.

It is time for a truly democratic vision of the heavenly, ever-present Father/Mother God to unite all of us, to inspire and lift us as a nation and a people beyond the sociology, beyond the biology, beyond the limitations of the day and into newness of life.

It is time for us all to witness the joys of Creation and to leave behind us the codependent past.

The happy ending, the message of this book, the message of the Twelve Step programs, the message of the churches, is that faith—a trusting exploration of the Higher Power—is the happiest of all endings and the only story worth telling and worth listening for. The message that there is a sacred self, a spiritual identity crying out to be heard is the message that is put into practice when the voice of the codependent yields to the "still, small voice" of God that breaks the spell of codependency and ushers in God dependency.

Part Two

The Workbook

"Behold, I will bring them complete recovery and healing and will reveal to them abundance of peace and security." (Jeremiah 33:6, AT)

"I am the Lord that healeth thee." (Exodus 15:26, AV)

How to Use The Workbook

"Behold, the Lord passed by, and a great and strong wind rent the mountains, and brake in pieces the rocks before the Lord; but the Lord was not in the wind: and after the wind an earthquake; but the Lord was not in the earthquake: and after the earthquake a fire; but the Lord was not in the fire: and after the fire a still small voice." (1Kings 19:11–12, AV)

This section of the book is a workbook section. It takes some of the symptoms and issues prevalent in the minds of codependents and applies what the Bible says to those symptoms. The Bible is full of healings of all kinds of demons, and is fraught with examples of casting out the suffering caused by codependent behavior.

The workbook addresses the *I*, the self, that feels separated from Love, Spirit, Truth, God, the Higher Power. The personal pronouns are in italics for emphasis in claiming these texts as personal and applicable to your own situation and life—for getting to know something of the nature of God described in the Bible.

Use the workbook to become familiar with the Bible; use it to discover your relationship to God as shown in the Judeo-Christian texts. Use it to overcome feelings of worthlessness and confusion. Use it for yourself or as a discussion tool with friends. Use it as a suggested start for more study.

The healing of codependency—or any life problem—is not necessarily found in the letter of the law, but in the spirit. The spirit of the texts and their relevance to a wounded self is intact. Perhaps, seeing the texts in a new light will provoke your thought and strengthen your faith.

These biblical statements on the following pages and

their application to the symptoms of codependency are suggestions to think about and reflect upon. They are not meant to be formulas or mantras. Each individual will find his or her own texts, his or her own thoughts on what the Bible has to say through personal reflection and study. There are many thoughts in the Bible which apply to each symptom or problem. The ones suggested here will probably lead you to others that you will find even more revealing. Each individual should find for him or herself what texts from the Old or New Testament apply to their specific situation or feelings. This can be done in a group setting or by yourself. If you think you are easily influenced you might prefer to use this section privately.

Those who are not familiar with accessing the Bible and its specific applications to daily life will find a Bible Concordance helpful. A bookstore should be able to provide you with a Bible Concordance. *Strong's Exhaustive Concordance of the Bible* (Nashville, Tenn.: Thomas Nelson, 1984) was used for the research in this book.

There are many different translations of the Bible in English. *The Authorized King James Version*; *The New Testament in Modern English*, J. B. Phillips, translator; *The Amplified Bible*; and *The Bible: An American Translation* were used for this book as was *Tanakh-The Holy Scriptures*: *The New JPS Translation According to the Traditional Hebrew Text* for some of the references from the Psalms. One might also explore the *New American Bible* and the *New Jerusalem Bible* for references. Different translations yield different inferences in the original texts, and the point is to find which one speaks to you and makes sense to you in your experience and life. Finding a translation and interpretation that makes sense to you is part of the process of discovering spiritual self-reliance.

If you are not familiar with the Bible you may wonder

what some of the texts in this section of the book have to do with the issues of codependency. But if one of them strikes you it may encourage you to find others in the Bible that have real meaning for you.

If you are learned in the Bible and have a very fixed understanding and perspective on interpreting scripture you may react to some of the following selections with the feeling that they are being misused—that, in fact, they mean something else. These texts do not quarrel with other interpretations of them, and the goal of this book is not to interpret Scripture. It is to appreciate the relevance of the Bible to the specific problems of any individual.

Preparing to hear the still small voice that says about yourself, *I am* every good thought, every good deed, every loving action that *I* ever had, felt warm about, acted upon, is what the following section of this book is about.

The focus of Part Two is on how to recognize that healing is true for *you*; how to turn your sense of *yourself* from something unworthy, unloved, confused, adrift, abandoned into a sense of *you* as full of goodness and power.

In the words of an Alcoholics Anonymous motto, "Take what you want and leave the rest behind."

In the words of 1 John 4:1, "Try the spirits."

THE SACRED SELF

"Before I formed thee in the belly I knew thee; and before thou camest forth out of the womb I sanctified thee."

(Jeremiah 1:5, AV)

My individuality is found in Soul. Soul is that sense that *I am* and *I'm* pretty terrific and *I* want to feel like this all the time.

I am the one that wants to know about Creation. *I* am the one who is tired of dead rationales. *I* am the one who needs to know how and when *I* was created. *I* want to know *my* timeless, spiritual identity, *my* real name as the child of the Living Father and Mother of us all. *I* want to know where *I* came from. *I* want to find peace. *My* holy, sacred self is in place and *I* want to see that self here and now.

Ask yourself—Do I believe God created me? Do I believe I have a right to know God?

ACCOMPLISHMENT

"So shall my word be that goeth forth out of my mouth: it shall not return unto me void, but it shall accomplish that which I please, and it shall prosper in the thing whereto I sent it. For ye shall go out with joy, and be led forth with peace."
(Isaiah 55:11–13, AV)

Your words are for everyone at every time. At this moment it doesn't matter what *I* have done or been through. At this moment all *I* need is to listen quietly. You know what leads *me* to peace. You will show *me* Your Creation and all its blessings.

I am the one who wants to know the Word and how it affects *my* life. *I* am the one who feels *I* can't express myself and *I'd* like to know the Word that would heal that problem and loose *my* tongue to say only the honest truth. *I* am the one that needs the pleasure of accomplishment of *my* true purpose. *I* want to feel joy. *I* want to know peace. *I* want to enter into the all the benefits of Your joy. *I* will follow Your leadings.

Your thoughts—Your Word—settles the issues of *my* life.

Ask yourself—Is God's work finished? Is God in control?

ASKING AND RECEIVING

"Ask, and it shall be given you; seek, and ye shall find; knock, and it shall be opened unto you."

(Luke 11:9, AV)

I ask and *I* receive it, *I* look for it and *I* find it, *I* knock and doors open.

It is *my* right to depend on that.

I am not paralyzed. *I* am active.

You, the Creator, alone create. *I* cannot create anything unlike you. *I* cannot create fear. *I* cannot create hate. *I* cannot create codependency. *I* am too busy minding *my* own business.

I am so busy asking You to show *me* all that is mine and so busy seeking and enjoying Creation that there is not enough time for inactivity, not enough time for dread, not enough time for sorrow.

Ask yourself—Am I asking God to change me or someone else?

THE NATURE OF GOD AND SELF

Counsel is mine; and sound wisdom
"I am understanding; I have strength."
(Proverbs 8:14, AV)

I am related to I Am. *I* will know *my* identity. *I* think about *my* I Amness. *I* claim my right to be one with I Am.

I am something. *I* am somebody.

I understand who You are as *I* listen, look for and feel Your presence.

I understand myself as *I* look to You, *my* Creator.

Understanding Your power and *mine* gives *me* courage and strength.

Ask yourself—What am I trying to understand? How does my understanding of God influence this search?

GOD AS FATHER

*"Have we not all one father? Did not
one God create us ?"*

(Malachi 2:10, AT)

God is *my* Father. He conceived *me* and *I* look like Spirit and *I* obey Spirit and *I* follow after spiritual things.

I can examine myself, making a searching moral inventory of *my* resentments toward *my* father, *my* dependence on *my* relationship with him; and *I* can see how *my* dependence on *my* father for happiness blots out a sense of You as Impartial Father.

My father cannot manipulate *me* in memory or in this day.

My Father knows what things *I* need before *I* ask.

I am not divorced from *my* Father, Spirit.

I am not a lost child wandering from place to place looking for *my* father, trying to fulfill his demands. *My* Father sees me when *I* am a long way off and meets *me* where *I* am on *my* journey. He clothes *me* with the thoughts that comfort *me*. He forgives *me* because he sees *me* as ever one with Creation.

I can only inherit from *my* Father, God.

Make a list of qualities that you associate with God as you understand Him. Make a list of qualities that your father represents to you. Where do they overlap? Should they?

GOD AS MOTHER

*"As one whom his mother comforteth,
so will I comfort you."*

(Isaiah 66:13, AV)

I am not an accident. *I* am not a burden to a Mother who has infinite compassion and love and resources.

I inherit all good from *my* Mother. Your arms are around *me*, You will never let *me* stray nor put *me* in danger. You do not limit *me*. You are a shield to *me*. You give *me* strength all the days of *my* life and *I* can turn to You whenever *I* need to. You are always there and nothing can obscure true Motherhood from *my* eyes.

Make a list of the qualities of God as Mother. Make a list of your mother's qualities. Compare them. Where do they overlap? Should they?

PRAYER AND PERCEPTION

> *"Now Hannah, she spake in her heart;*
> *only her lips moved, but her voice was not heard:*
> *therefore Eli thought she had been drunken. And*
> *Eli said unto her, How long wilt thou be drunken?*
> *put away thine wine from thee. And Hannah*
> *answered and said, No, my lord, I am a woman*
> *of a sorrowful spirit: I have drunk neither wine nor*
> *strong drink, but have poured out my soul before*
> *the Lord."*
>
> (1 Samuel 1:13–15, AV)

I know what *I* am doing. It doesn't matter what others think if *I* am turning to God—You—as best as *I* know how.

I'm right if *I* am relating to my Higher Power. *I* am wrong when *I* am not relating to *my* Higher Power.

I know how to say No.

I am not Eve. *I* am wisdom.

I take no joy in manipulation.

I take no joy in being manipulated.

I want to live in the Light of Love

I will not, cannot live anywhere else.

You are always in *my* thoughts.

Ask yourself—Do I care what God thinks? Do God's thoughts coincide with mine? Should they?

COUPLES AND CODEPENDENCY

> *"In the beginning God created the heaven and the earth.*
>
> *So God created man in his own image, in the image of God created he him; male and female created he them.*
>
> *And God saw every thing that he had made, and, behold, it was very good."*
>
> (Genesis 1:1, 27, 31, AV)

There is no codependency in spiritual creation.

Codependency in couples is a parody of spiritual Creation and spiritual self-reliance.

Ownership is the standard for property but not for persons. Suffering ends when codependency ends. Shame and guilt disappear when codependency is gone.

Make a list of what you want out of a relationship that is troubling you. Make a list of what you are willing to give. Are the expectations and what you are willing to give equal? Close to equal?

SILENCING THE CODEPENDENT NARRATIVE

"Be still, and know that I am God."
(Psalm 46:10, AV)

I am pulled back and forth, up and down by *my* relationships. *I* wonder what s/he thinks. *I* wonder what will happen next, *I* wonder if s/he will disappoint *me*, fulfill *me*, please *me*, praise *me*, provoke *me*.

I hate it when *I* feel this way. *I* remind myself that *I* am God dependent. *I* am one with *my* Higher Power. *I* reflect the individuality of God and *I* am not dependent on any other power, past or future.

Love gives *me* nourishment, grace, freedom. Truth does not belittle *me*. Soul respects *me* and *I* respect *myself*.

Ask yourself—Can I listen to God for one minute? Two?

COMPANIONSHIP

"Thou art ever with me, and all that I have is thine."

(Luke 15:31, AV)

All the Motherhood and Fatherhood of God is *mine* at this moment and no past loss can make *me* believe otherwise. *I* stand at the door of a new day and no one can shut out the light.

I refuse to let any man or woman cause *me* to grovel, complain, cry or moan.

Spirit is *my* Comforter.

I am not afraid of any loss of codependency. There is nothing that *I* have that is good that Love does not provide. Nothing that is bad will survive the Truth that the Higher Power alone orders and controls *my* experience.

Ask yourself—What will happen if I let go of a bad relationship? Will God forget me?

DOMINION

*"And there appeared a great wonder in heaven;
a woman clothed with the sun, and the moon
under her feet, and upon her head a crown of
twelve stars."*

(Revelation 12:1, AV)

I will refuse to see *myself* as separate from God. *I* reflect Creation. *I* know God as Love, as Truth, as compassionate and patient and merciful and tolerant and endlessly forbearing.

I will not give power to anyone else when power belongs to God. Spiritual strength is *my* right.

God loves men and women as individual ideas of Her presence and *I* am an individual idea of God's presence and *I* am, therefore, loved.

I will not be used by envy, jealousy, greed, false pride, or false power. *I* will not ask any person to be God. *I* will let God supply *me* with proper companionship and comfort in God's own way.

Ask yourself—Am I on top of my moods?

ABANDONMENT

"I will not leave you comfortless."
(John 14:18, AV)

What a word: Abandonment.

Abandonment is one of the great fears of those in the Twelve Step meetings, and of many others of us as well. The children of alcoholics feel abandoned. They fear being left; they fear attachment for fear of being left or abandoned. It has happened to them before, it can happen again; it will happen again; and no matter how they try, they cannot trust with constancy. They cannot trust others, they cannot trust themselves. The home that they should feel inside themselves is insecure and empty.

But *I* am never abandoned by Spirit. *I* can enlarge my sense of what being taken care of means. *I* can start being at home now with *my* self and with You.

Make a list of people and institutions that you feel have abandoned you. Make a list of people you have abandoned.

COMFORT

*"Lo, I am with you alway, even unto the
end of the world."*
(Matthew 28:20, AV)

Recognizing *my* feelings is the first thing *I* do.
I am disquieted, irrational, afraid. *I'm* trying to fill up the
empty space with _____.
No.
I can and *I* will replace *my* symptoms of fear, of hope-
lessness with spiritual facts.
Divine Love never abandons the Loved. Love is universal, and Love is specific. Love is not lost, love is everywhere,
in everything good and beautiful and true. Love is eternal not
temporal.
Love surrounds *me* and does not leave *me*. *I* can, *I* am
able to open *my* eyes and see love in *my* daily life. *I* am
spiritually self-reliant. *I* am comforted now and always.

Ask yourself—When was the last time I felt comforted? The
first time?

LOVE

"We love him, because he first loved us."

(1 John 4:19, AV)

"Let us love one another, for love comes from God, and everyone who loves is a child of God and knows God."

(1 John 4:7, AT)

The comings and goings of *my* loved ones take place in Love. Love comes to them and to *me*. *I* have a right to an emotionally secure and practical and spiritual home where *I am* at rest in peace and quiet and comfort.

I can know that God loves me and *my* loved ones. Because Love loves me *I* love *myself* (and everyone else) in the wisdom of Love.

Ask yourself—Does Love know walls, boundaries, limits?

SHAME

> *"Ye shall not be ashamed nor*
> *confounded world without end. "*
>   (Isaiah 45:17, AV)

What am *I* ashamed of? Adam? Eve? Being human?
My father, *my* mother? *My* children? *My* response to them?
My inappropriate response to those closest to *me*? Far from
me?
   I will not hide in shame.
   I am not ashamed to be Your child.
   I am not ashamed to be *me*.

Make a list that separates shame for your actions from shame
that is projected on you by others. Make amends for your own
actions. Refuse to accept shame or blame that others put on
you.

ONE GOD

"Thou shalt have no other gods before me."

(Exodus 20:3, AV)

There is only One Infinite Life, Truth and there is no other. This Truth speaks to *me* directly. This Life lives through *me* immediately and directly and in simple, loving ways. This Truth is clear and makes itself known to *me* in *my* most inward parts. The One I Am, Life, Truth, is the only voice that *I* can hear, the only impulsion for *my* actions.

I am not the slave of another's thoughts.

The only impulsion for *my* actions is the One I Am.

I refuse to make many gods by constantly talking about others.

Ask yourself—How many gods live in my house?

CARETAKING

"Take therefore no thought for the morrow: for the morrow shall take thought for the things of itself."

(Matthew 6:34, AV)

Identities are not found, but lost in continually taking care of those who are old enough to take care of themselves.

I love serving in the Spirit of Truth, in the Presence of the sacred, but *I* hate picking up after grown people.

God cares for the fowls of the air and the lilies of the field and God takes care of *me*. God cares for every thing and everyone in Creation.

There is no force of will that can keep *me* from seeing that *I* am cared for. No demands of any self—*mine* or another's—can keep *me* from seeing the Higher Power of all life as infinite, impartial Love.

Ask yourself—Do I do a better job than God of taking care? Am I putting myself in the place of God?

CONTROL

> *"Who hath ascended up into heaven, or*
> *descended? Who hath gathered the wind in his*
> *fists? Who hath bound the waters in a garment?*
> *Who hath established all the ends of the earth?*
> *What is his name, and what is his son's name, if*
> *thou canst tell?"*
>
> (Proverbs 30:4, AV)

"Letting go and letting God" is okay if *I* know who God is. Otherwise, it's only a slogan. Because an all-good, all-powerful God is in control, *I* control only *my* thoughts and actions. *I* am not interested in controlling others.

Make a list of who you wish would control you. Who you wish wouldn't. Why you think it would be fine to be controlled or control.

CONFUSION

*"For the Lord will not forsake his people;
He will not abandon his heritage."*
                                        (Psalm 94:14, RSV)

I am blown about by emotions and thoughts that have nothing in them that will give *me* peace.

My soul longeth for the courts of the living God.

I am not afraid to recognize the emptiness of falsehoods, of lies, of promises not kept. *I* can and will repent, change *my* thinking, press on.

I am, in fact related to God alone.

God's company gives *me* grace, peace, comfort.

I am not confused. You direct *me*. *I* rely on Your clarity.

Ask yourself—Can I trust that God knows what makes sense?

FULFILLMENT

*"Neither shall they say, Lo here!
or, lo there! for, behold, the kingdom of
God is within you."*

(Luke 17:21, AV)

I am not adrift on the stormy sea of unfulfilled romance.

I am not using sex or being used sexually to mask feelings of abandonment. *I* deserve only to see the control of Love and *I* deserve the chance to know *my* spiritual self.

Love is not stagnant. Love is ever active. Love cuts through self doubt, possessiveness and fear. Love cuts through feelings of emptiness and the recurrent shadows of abandonment and shows *me* where God is being expressed now in *my* life.

Ask yourself—Where is God in my life?

NEVER TOO LATE

*"Behold, now is the accepted time;
behold, now is the day of salvation. "*
(2 Corinthians 6:2, AV)

I am grateful. *I* can count the things that are terrible that have happened to *me*. The wonderful things are too many to count and *I* am learning them now.

This moment is one in a day of moments. Each moment is a reflection of all the Good that *I* can assimilate at this time.

I am not plotting out *my* life of horrors.

I am enjoying this moment.

Regardless of the past *I am* living now and *I* know the difference between Life and drama.

Make a list of things for which you are grateful. Can you add to the list one thing for each day, week, month, year?

GRATITUDE

"Father, I thank thee that thou hast heard me. And I knew that thou hearest me always."

(John 11:41–42, AV)

Gratitude is not up there some place. Gratitude is friends who remember, strangers who smile, women picking children up at school, car pools, swimming pools, hot bread. Gratitude is real. *I* can be grateful before *I* am well. *I* can be grateful in a mess. *I* am grateful for the idea of You.

Make a list of people for which you are grateful. It can be anyone. Start with one person. Add to the list daily, then hourly. Be grateful and accept good.

DISCERNMENT

"For the word of God is quick, and powerful, and sharper than any twoedged sword, piercing even to the dividing asunder of soul and spirit, and of the joints and marrow, and is a discerner of the thoughts and intents of the heart."

(Hebrews 4:12, AV)

I have every right to know—now—what to do this minute. *I* can tell who means *me* well and who does not. *I* refuse to be naive or seduced. *I* refuse to accept any notion that education or experience is the only way to know what is happening. *I* know that God will reveal to *me* what *I* need to know. *I* will look to the heart and to purity.

Make a list of your spiritual qualities: the ones that come from God and that are yours by virtue of your relationship to Life, Truth, Spirit. Put it up on the mirror and look at it as a guide to who you are.

FORCES OTHER THAN MYSELF

*"For we wrestle not against flesh and
blood, but against principalities, against powers,
against the rulers of the darkness of this world,
against spiritual wickedness in high places."*
(Ephesians 6:12, AV)

I realize that everything is not about *me* but about all of
us. *I* am grateful for daily reminders of that fact.

My life sounds like the lyrics to a country and western
song. *I* want it to sound like a song of praise. *I'd* better stop
thinking about *myself* as a victim and listen instead to some
spiritual sounds.

I am not the center of the universe.

There is a Higher Power.

I trust that.

Make a list of who and what you trust. See if it changes as
you learn more about God in your life.

PROTECTION FOR THE VULNERABLE

"The Lord watches over the strangers;
the orphan and widow he supports."
(Psalm 146:9, AT)

I will not feel sorry for *myself* if *I* am alone or powerless. *I* will not rehearse self-pity. The I Am is watching over *me*. God gives strength and courage to the widows and orphans, to the poor and powerless and comes to *me* when *I* am weakest and most in need. God is not in the accumulation of goods but in the very lives of those who most need Love.

Ask yourself—Do I believe I deserve God in my life?

ADDICTION

*"Why art thou cast down, O my soul?
And why art thou disquieted within me? Hope
thou in God: for I shall yet praise him, who is the
health of my countenance, and my God."*
(Psalms 42:11, AV)

There is a contagion in the air that says if you are not high on something, some acquisition, some rush that clouds judgment, some moment in time alone and unconnected to all other moments, then you are not really living.

Substance abuse means what it says. We all abuse the idea of true substance. True substance is faith that God provides all good for the daughters and sons of Creation.

Make a list of your addictions: Coffee, tea, self-righteousness, loneliness, emptiness, television, noise, drama, excitement, self-pity, fear are a few current addictions. Which ones will you break now?

And of course, there is always the . . .

LIST FOR THE REFRIGERATOR

1. I listen for You.
2. I keep an open mind.
3. I do not let another define God for me.
4. I define God for myself.
5. I search the Scriptures for definitions of You.
6. I ask questions.
7. I study and inquire and I learn.
8. I am not lazy about finding You.
9. I put into practice what I hear, what I learn, what I know each and every day.
10. I look for evidence of You not in words but in changes in my life.

"Finally, brethren, whatsoever things are true, whatsoever things are honest, whatsoever things are just, whatsoever things are pure, whatsoever things are lovely, whatsoever things are of good report; if there be any virtue, and if there be any praise, think on these things."

(Philippians 4:8, AV)

Conclusion

Two people, two interviews that I conducted over a decade ago stick in my mind as I write the conclusion to this book.

One of them was an interview with Jean-Christophe Oberg, the then Swedish Ambassador to Thailand.

We were having tea in his office in Bangkok one afternoon and we were talking about Vietnam and the world perception of that country and of the U.S. involvement there.

The war in Vietnam split nations, split psyches and destroyed and changed lives—without respect to nationality.

"You know," he said, reflecting "there are worse things than political tyranny. The tyranny of the family is one of those things."

I wasn't sure that I agreed with him at the time but I heard his words resonate in my ears. I knew, in a way, that he was right.

For some people, living in the tyranny of an addicted home is war. It takes its innocent victims just as surely as do bombs.

A few years later I interviewed a woman, Martha Ann Baumer, who was then a minister for the United Church of Christ, serving a southwestern town. She was wearing jeans and cowboy boots and a pullover when we talked one afternoon in my office and what she told me that day still rings in my ears.

"A lot of people say to me," she said, "that church failed them when they were younger and so they have no interest in going back. And I ask them," she continued, " 'Have you tried it as an adult, have you tried it as you are now, at 30 or 40 or whatever, as a married person or a person who has some larger sense of the world?'"

What Jean-Christophe Oberg and Marty Baumer said ten years ago seems to me today to apply to all the issues of addiction and codependency.

There is a tyranny of the family. And what we were, what we knew, what we did as children is not what we can do, are able to do, or should be doing as adults.

Our childhood disappointments, our perceptions at those times can be turned into the joys of knowing ourselves as full adults. Things have changed.

We have changed, our needs have changed.

Families have changed, or we can change them.

Church has changed, or we can change it.

We are not helpless victims of our past.

We should not allow ourselves to be stuck in our memories. We should not allow ourselves to be left with less than we deserve of God's love and mercy and justice.

Codependency and addiction remind us that it is hell to live in perpetual trauma and powerlessness. It is hell to suffer for someone else's failings.

And there is nothing in heaven or earth that says this is the way that it must be.

In fact, there is evidence to the contrary.

Many people—not enough, but many—have been released from terrible slavery as political prisoners. Many people condemned to die have been released to entirely new lives.

It has happened to them. It can happen to you.

But why one is saved and not another is not something that someone who is suffering can afford the luxury of debating. Suffering cries out for relief.

In wartime it is easy to point the finger at who is to blame—although there are usually forces behind the forces. In addiction it is also easy to point the blame. Some of us suffer because of other people's addictions and it is no more just than a monsoon or a tidal wave.

When thinking about codependency I kept coming back to addiction. To liquor or drugs. It is difficult to look at the issue of codependency without the realization that if there were no alcohol abuse, no chemical substance abuse, there would be no discussion of codependency. Addiction. Addiction makes addicts and it makes codependents.

There would still be, in some circles, the issue of addiction in churches. There would still be people who are hurt by other people's thoughtless and driven actions. There would still be the issue of understanding God for yourself.

Addiction and codependency are among the painful issues raised by the tyranny of the family and by society. But the point is not to blame—but to seek God for yourself.

God is not in the collective conscience of a church or a nation unless it is in the individual conscience of each one of us.

Bringing an understanding of God into your life can turn codependency into spiritual self-reliance and can change the perspective of the family, the church and the nation.

God, acknowledged and sought, is a source of strength to the individual, a very present help in trouble, and in the end, all there is.

A Proposal for Churches

(Adapted From the Twelve Steps and the Twelve Traditions)

1. Our common welfare should come first: personal recovery depends on church unity.

2. For our group purpose there is but one ultimate authority—a loving God as God may express the I Am of our church conscience. Our leaders are to be trusted servants; they do not govern.

3. The only requirement for church membership is a desire to be healed.

4. Each group should be autonomous except in matters affecting other groups or the church as a whole.

5. Each church has but one primary purpose—to carry its message to the individual who still suffers.

6. A church ought never endorse, finance, or lend the church name to any related facility or outside enterprise, lest problems of money, property, and prestige divert us from our primary purpose.

7. Every church ought to be fully self-supporting, declining outside contributions.

8. Our church should remain forever non-professional, but our service centers may employ special workers.

9. Church, as such, should never be organized; but we may create service boards or committees directly responsible to those they serve.

10. Our church has no opinion on outside issues; hence the church name ought never to be drawn into public controversy.

11. Our public relations policy is based on attraction rather than promotion; we need always maintain personal anonymity at the level of press, radio, films, and television.

12. Anonymity is the spiritual foundation of all our Traditions, ever reminding us to place the principle of one infinite all-loving God before personalities.

The Lord's Prayer and the Twelve Steps

The Twelve Steps of Alcoholics Anonymous are synonymous with the sentiments in the Lord's Prayer. Here is one way to look at them as resonating together.

OUR FATHER WHICH ART IN HEAVEN, HALLOWED BE THY NAME.

We admitted we were powerless over alcohol—that our lives had become unmanageable (1); we came to believe that a power greater than ourselves could restore us to sanity (2).

THY KINGDOM COME. THY WILL BE DONE IN EARTH, AS IT IS IN HEAVEN.

We believe that, and so we made a decision to turn our will and our lives over to the care of God as we understand God (3).

GIVE US THIS DAY OUR DAILY BREAD.

Leave us not unnourished and unloved. Restore our innocence and our hope and our love of truth. We know that to ignorantly worship God is to miss the zest and joy of living that you want for us. And so, to obtain the bread of truth that you have so generously provided for us, we made a searching and fearless moral inventory of ourselves (4). We admitted to God, to ourselves, and to another human being the exact nature of our wrongs (5), and were entirely ready to have God remove all these defects of character (6). We humbly asked You to remove our shortcomings (7).

AND FORGIVE US OUR DEBTS, AS WE FORGIVE OUR DEBTORS.

We made a list of all persons we had harmed, and became willing to make amends to them all (8); We made direct amends to such people wherever possible, except when to do so would injure them or others (9); and we continued to take personal inventory, and when we were wrong promptly admitted it (10). We remembered.

AND LEAD US NOT INTO TEMPTATION, BUT DELIVER US FROM EVIL.

We remembered and sought through prayer and meditation to improve our conscious contact with you as we understand you, praying only for the knowledge of your will for us and power to carry that out (11).

FOR THINE IS THE KINGDOM AND THE POWER AND THE GLORY FOREVER.

Having had a spiritual awakening as a result of these steps, we tried to carry this message to others and to practice these principles in our affairs (12).

There are many ways to find relationships between the Twelve Steps and the Lord's Prayer. Look deeply into both and see what strikes you as coincidental. What form would you use to show the relationship between them? How can you apply the Lord's Prayer to your specific problems?